Hannah Stevens

Bread and Circuses
Emotional Projection and Social Behavior

Original Title: *Bread and Circuses*

Copyright © 2025, published by Luiz Antonio dos Santos ME.

This book is a non-fiction work that explores the impact of emotional projection and social behavior in the modern era. The author examines how collective symbols, narratives, and entertainment shape public perception and influence emotions and individual decisions.

1st Edition

Production Team

Author: Hannah Stevens

Editor: Luiz Santos

Cover Design: Studios Booklas / *Nathan Carter*

Consultant: *Robert Mendel*

Researchers: *Eleanor Hayes, Jonathan Blake, Sofia Mendez*

Typesetting: *Lucas Ferrell*

Publication and Identification

Bread and Circuses

Booklas, 2025

Categories: Social Psychology / Collective Behavior

DDC: 302.1 | **CDU:** 316.6

All rights reserved to:

Luiz Antonio dos Santos ME / Booklas

No part of this book may be reproduced, stored in a retrieval system, or transmitted by any means—electronic, mechanical, photocopying, recording, or otherwise—without prior written permission from the copyright holder.

Summary

Systematic Index 5
Prologue 9
Chapter 1 The Illusion of Conquest 12
Chapter 2 The History of Bread and Circuses 18
Chapter 3 The Brain and Emotion Addiction 24
Chapter 4 Psychology of the Crowd 30
Chapter 5 The Impact on Individual Identity 36
Chapter 6 The Power of Narratives 42
Chapter 7 The Political Use of Emotion 48
Chapter 8 The Herd Effect 55
Capítulo 9 As Redes Sociais e a Nova Arena 61
Chapter 10 The Role of the Media 68
Chapter 11 The Culture of Entertainment 75
Chapter 12 The Cult of Celebrity 81
Chapter 13 Fanaticism and Extremism 87
Chapter 14 The Price of Alienation 93
Chapter 15 The Relationship with Social Class 100
Chapter 16 Exceptions to the Rule 106
Chapter 17 The Illusion of Control 113
Chapter 18 How to Break the Cycle 119
Chapter 19 Emotional Minimalism 125
Chapter 20 The Power of Self-Responsibility 131
Chapter 21 The High-Performance Mind 136

Chapter 22 How to Reprogram Your Mind 141
Chapter 23 The Art of Detachment 147
Chapter 24 Creating Your Own Narrative 152
Chapter 25 Rescuing Emotional Control 157
Chapter 26 The New Model of Thinking 162
Chapter 27 The World Without Illusions 167
Chapter 28 Breaking Free from the Circus 173
Epilogue 180

Systematic Index

Chapter 1: The Illusion of Conquest - Explores how emotional projection influences social behavior, creating an illusion of participation in external events.

Chapter 2: The History of Bread and Circuses - Discusses the historical use of "Bread and Circuses" as a strategy for social control, from ancient Rome to modern societies.

Chapter 3: The Brain and Emotion Addiction - Explores the neurological basis of emotional addiction, explaining how the brain's reward system is manipulated by external stimuli.

Chapter 4: Psychology of the Crowd - Analyzes how individuals are influenced by crowd dynamics, including deindividuation, emotional contagion, and suggestibility.

Chapter 5: The Impact on Individual Identity - Discusses how external stimuli and emotional dependence can compromise personal identity and self-esteem.

Chapter 6: The Power of Narratives - Explores the role of narratives in shaping perceptions, influencing emotions, and driving social behavior.

Chapter 7: The Political Use of Emotion - Analyzes how emotions are strategically used in politics to manipulate public opinion and maintain power.

Chapter 8: The Herd Effect - Discusses the psychological phenomenon of individuals following the behavior of the majority, often without critical thinking.

Chapter 9: As Redes Sociais e a Nova Arena (Social Networks and the New Arena) - Examines the impact of social networks on communication, information consumption, and emotional engagement.

Chapter 10: The Role of the Media - Discusses the media's role in shaping public opinion, constructing narratives, and manipulating emotions.

Chapter 11: The Culture of Entertainment - Analyzes how entertainment influences perceptions, behaviors, and emotions, functioning as a tool for social influence.

Chapter 12: The Cult of Celebrity - Discusses the phenomenon of celebrity worship and its effects on individuals and society.

Chapter 13: Fanaticism and Extremism - Analyzes the psychological roots and social consequences of fanaticism and extremism.

Chapter 14: The Price of Alienation - Discusses the personal and social costs of alienation caused by excessive immersion in distractions.

Chapter 15: The Relationship with Social Class - Examines how social class influences the relationship with entertainment-driven alienation and access to opportunities.

Chapter 16: Exceptions to the Rule - Discusses how emotional involvement with mass entertainment and external events transcends social classes.

Chapter 17: The Illusion of Control - Explores the psychological phenomenon of believing one has influence over external events.

Chapter 18: How to Break the Cycle - Provides strategies for individuals to break free from the cycle of emotional manipulation and distraction.

Chapter 19: Emotional Minimalism - Introduces the concept of emotional minimalism as a way to manage emotional overload in modern life.

Chapter 20: The Power of Self-Responsibility - Emphasizes the importance of taking personal responsibility for one's emotional reactions and well-being.

Chapter 21: The High-Performance Mind - Explores the characteristics and habits of high-performance individuals.

Chapter 22: How to Reprogram Your Mind - Discusses techniques for changing thought patterns and limiting beliefs.

Chapter 23: The Art of Detachment - Emphasizes the importance of emotional detachment for achieving inner peace and balance.

Chapter 24: Creating Your Own Narrative - Encourages individuals to define their own path and create a personal narrative aligned with their values.

Chapter 25: Rescuing Emotional Control - Provides guidance on regaining control over one's emotions and achieving emotional autonomy.

Chapter 26: The New Model of Thinking - Presents a new model of thinking focused on conscious choices, discernment, and intentionality.

Chapter 27: The World Without Illusions - Imagines the potential transformations in society if individuals were free from illusions and manipulation.

Chapter 28: Breaking Free from the Circus - Concludes the book by summarizing key themes and encouraging readers to take control of their lives.

Prologue

Human society has always been guided by shared symbols, narratives, and emotions. From great empires to the hyperconnected world, the need for belonging and validation has been one of the main drivers of collective behavior. Spectacle has always been an efficient tool for distraction and control, and its modern form manifests itself in social media, mass entertainment, cycles of political outrage, and sports and ideological rivalries. The essence remains the same: to keep the public's attention directed toward carefully planned stimuli, while the true centers of power operate without significant resistance.

Humans are driven by emotions, but to what extent are these emotions truly their own? The addiction to external stimuli – whether in politics, sports, or digital culture – creates a cycle where individual identity is shaped by external events and figures. The triumph of an idol, the defeat of an opponent, or the virality of a new trend dictate the mood and daily concerns of millions, often to the detriment of genuine experiences and personal development. The illusion of collective achievement replaces individual victories, and the sense of belonging overrides the search for autonomy and meaning.

The digital age has amplified this phenomenon by creating systems that not only capture but also direct the attention of the masses. Algorithms monitor and shape behaviors, reinforce beliefs, and feed thought bubbles, making exposure to contradictory viewpoints increasingly difficult. Public debate fragments, polarization intensifies, and society divides into groups that react impulsively to emotional stimuli designed to generate engagement. The goal is not to inform or generate reflection, but to keep people trapped in the cycle of euphoria and indignation, ensuring their participation in the spectacle, but not in real decision-making power.

The manipulation of collective attention does not only occur in the field of politics or entertainment. Large corporations use the same strategies to transform emotions into consumption, desires into profits, and personal identity into a reflection of market-dictated trends. Individuality is diluted in pre-fabricated lifestyles, and freedom becomes a well-sold illusion. While crowds lose themselves in carefully crafted distractions, decisions that impact society in a concrete way are made without significant resistance.

However, understanding this process is already a step towards freeing oneself from it. Knowledge about the mechanisms of social influence, emotional triggers, and cycles of manipulation allows one to regain control over what really deserves attention. In a world where distraction is the norm, cultivating the ability to reflect, question, and direct one's own energy towards authentic goals is an act of resistance.

This does not mean rejecting entertainment, popular culture, or social engagement, but developing a more conscious relationship with these experiences. It means seeing the spectacle for what it is without becoming hostage to it. It means recognizing when intense emotions are genuine and when they are induced. It means valuing achievements that are born from personal effort, instead of getting lost in symbolic victories that add nothing to individual reality.

The world will always offer new forms of distraction, new idols to worship, and new causes to mobilize the masses. But true transformation does not happen in the spectacle. It happens in the choices of each individual who decides to regain control over their attention, their identity, and their own path. After all, the greatest freedom is not in escaping the system, but in seeing it clearly and consciously choosing what deserves space in one's own life.

Luiz Santos Editor.

Chapter 1
The Illusion of Conquest

Contemporary society is immersed in a network of stimuli that capture our attention and subtly shape our emotions. News, sports, entertainment, and social media act as triggers for intense sensations, causing us to experience euphoria or frustration in the face of events that, in practice, do not directly alter the course of our lives. But these reactions are not merely random or the result of superficial preferences. They reflect a deep psychological mechanism, rooted in the human need for belonging and identity.

Throughout history, social groups have been structured around symbols, rituals, and collective narratives that transcended the individual, creating a sense of unity and purpose. The same impulse that led ancient civilizations to identify with their clans and deities today manifests itself in the way we root for a team, follow the trajectory of a celebrity, or become emotionally involved in ideological debates. This emotional connection with external elements generates the illusion of participation, as if we were inserted in the events we observe. In reality, however, we are merely spectators, projecting our desires and frustrations onto figures and events alien to us.

The need for belonging drives the creation of symbolic bonds, which in turn influence the way we interpret reality. By identifying with a cause, a group, or a cultural icon, the individual finds a sense of community that transcends their individual existence. However, this emotional connection can end up serving as a mechanism of alienation, diverting the focus from personal experience to external entities. The victory of a soccer team, for example, can generate a feeling of personal glory as intense as a real achievement, while the defeat can be experienced as a personal tragedy. This process causes the person to constantly oscillate between exaltation and frustration, often without realizing that their happiness or anguish is being determined by factors completely beyond their control.

With the advancement of technology and the increase in virtual interactions, this dynamic has intensified even further. At every moment, we are bombarded by narratives that invite us to invest emotionally in distant events, reinforcing the feeling that we are, in some way, involved in them.

The illusion of conquest lies precisely in this transfer of emotions, in the belief that external victories and defeats reflect personal merits or failures. Although natural and historically consolidated, this projection can distance us from the authenticity of our own experiences. Over time, we learn to value symbols and representations more than our direct experiences, which influences our relationships, self-esteem, and perception of the world.

Understanding this phenomenon is essential to regaining control over our emotions and establishing a more balanced relationship with external stimuli. When we recognize that often our joy and frustration do not come from our own actions, but from a process of symbolic identification, we can free ourselves from the emotional trap that makes us feel triumphant or defeated by events that, ultimately, belong to others. This understanding does not mean giving up the passion for sports, culture, or ideologies, but rather developing a greater awareness of how these identifications affect our emotional well-being, allowing us to enjoy these experiences without being held hostage by their oscillations.

Since the dawn of civilization, human beings have demonstrated a remarkable ability to connect emotionally with abstract entities, symbols, and representations that go beyond the individual sphere. Tribes united under the protection of totems, nations were inflamed by flags and ideals, and communities vibrated together in rituals and celebrations. Far from being a mere whim, this behavior reflects a deep psychological mechanism, rooted in human evolution and essential to understanding the dynamics of modern societies.

This mechanism, which we can call emotional projection, occurs when we transfer our feelings, aspirations, and fears to external elements. Sports teams, celebrities, social movements, and even commercial brands can become vehicles for this projection. When we identify intensely with a soccer team, for example, we internalize its victories and defeats as if they were our own, feeling genuine joy in triumphs and bitterness in defeats. Similarly, idolatry for a celebrity can make us experience their successes and failures as extensions of our own lives, creating a sense of indirect connection with their trajectory.

Emotional projection, in itself, is not a negative thing. In its more balanced forms, it can strengthen social bonds, generate a sense of community, and provide moments of collective celebration. The problem arises when this tendency intensifies to the point that we become emotionally dependent on external events and symbols, overshadowing the value of our own experiences and achievements.

The illusion of conquest manifests itself precisely in this belief that the victories and defeats of external entities, with which we identify, are equivalent to personal achievements or failures. Fans who celebrate a sports title as if they had played or who are deeply saddened after a defeat illustrate this phenomenon. The intensity of the emotion is real, but its origin lies in a projection, in a displacement of feelings to an external object that, in essence, is not part of the individual's life.

This phenomenon is so present in everyday life that it often goes unnoticed. The passion for sports, which mobilizes crowds and provokes intense emotional reactions, is a classic example of emotional projection. Devotion to celebrities, transformed into icons of admiration and role models, follows the same pattern. Political and social movements, which generate ideological fervor and mobilize followers, often use this projection to strengthen the cohesion of their members and drive their causes.

In the digital age, this trend is amplified by the media and social networks. The spectacularization of sporting events, the glorification of the lives of celebrities, and the polarization of public debate create an ideal environment for the intensification of this psychological mechanism. Narratives carefully constructed to awaken emotions in the public reinforce this tendency to project our emotions onto external symbols.

This chapter aims to awaken in the reader the awareness that this dynamic is present in their daily lives, often unconsciously. The invitation here is to reflect on your own emotional reactions, question the sources of your joy and sadness, and analyze to what extent your emotions are being directed towards external events and symbols that, in practice, do not affect your life.

By recognizing this pattern, the chance arises to see our emotions and choices in a new way. Instead of being at the mercy of the oscillations caused by external events, we can direct our energy towards authentic experiences, building a sense of accomplishment that does not depend on other people's symbols or narratives. The passion for sports, admiration for public figures, and engagement in social causes can coexist with a more critical awareness, allowing us to enjoy these connections without giving up autonomy over our emotions.

This awakening does not require renouncing enthusiasm or excitement in the face of the world, but rather finding a healthy balance between involvement and detachment. When we understand that our identity does not need to rely on achievements that are not really ours, we can invest more time and energy in what truly enriches and transforms us. Thus, happiness ceases to be a reflection of uncontrollable factors and begins to be built from genuine and personal experiences.

The challenge lies in breaking with the inertia of this emotional conditioning and developing a more attentive look at what really defines us. If we recognize the difference between belonging and dependence, between involvement and alienation, we will be closer to a more emotionally stable and authentic life. After all, the true conquest is not in symbolic victories, but in the ability to find meaning and purpose within ourselves.

Chapter 2
The History of Bread and Circuses

The rise of great civilizations has always been linked to the need to maintain social order and ensure political stability. Since the earliest empires, rulers have realized that controlling the population could not rely solely on military force or strict laws. It was essential to offer something more: a balance between material satisfaction and entertainment, sufficient to keep the masses distracted and complacent, without questioning the power structures. This strategy, refined in Ancient Rome under the concept of "Bread and Circuses," was not only a political tool but also a reflection of the deep understanding of the psychological mechanisms that govern human behavior. The provision of essential goods, combined with grandiose spectacles, not only pacified the citizens but also kept them trapped in an illusion of well-being, diverting their attention from the most pressing issues of government and society.

The "Bread and Circuses" policy did not arise by chance but as a pragmatic response to the challenge of managing a vast and diverse society. Rome was a melting pot of cultures, where citizens, foreigners, slaves, and soldiers coexisted in a fragile dynamic. Keeping this structure functioning required more than military conquests or promises of prosperity. It was necessary to feed the population and, at the same time, offer an emotional outlet for the people to vent their frustrations without directing them against the government. The distribution of wheat at reduced prices or free of charge ensured the subsistence of the poorest, while the spectacles, organized in arenas like the Colosseum and the Circus Maximus, functioned as an efficient distraction. Far from being mere generous concessions, these strategies were a calculated means of social manipulation, ensuring that the population remained entertained and without motivation to challenge power.

The impact of this control model was so profound that its influence remains to this day, albeit in new forms. In the contemporary world, modern versions of "Bread and Circuses" continue to operate, but adapted to technological and cultural reality. Governments and large corporations understand that social stability depends not only on meeting basic needs but also on the constant supply of distractions. If gladiators once bled in the arena to entertain crowds, today sporting events, celebrity culture, the entertainment industry, and social media fulfill this same role, occupying the public's minds and emotions. Information circulates rapidly, but often without depth, functioning more as a distraction than as a tool for awareness. The Roman logic of transforming citizens into passive spectators is reflected in modern times, showing that "Bread and Circuses" not only survived but evolved with surprising efficiency.

At the heart of the Roman Empire, a vast territory spanning three continents, Rome pulsed as a metropolis full of contrasts and challenges. It was a place where opulence coexisted with poverty, power with vulnerability, and order with chaos. Governing this diverse population required more than military force and severe laws. It demanded a strategy capable of calming spirits, diverting attention from problems, and, above all, ensuring the loyalty of the population.

It was in this scenario that Roman leaders, endowed with political pragmatism and strategic insight, developed the formula of "Bread and Circuses." The essence of this strategy lay in the systematic offering of two essential elements for maintaining social peace: food and entertainment. "Bread" represented the free or subsidized distribution of wheat and other basic foodstuffs, guaranteeing the survival of the poorest and reducing the risk of revolts due to hunger and deprivation. "Circuses" encompassed a wide variety of public spectacles, from gladiator fights and chariot races to theatrical performances, athletic games, and religious festivities.

The spectacles, held in monumental arenas, gathered crowds and offered an escape from the harsh reality of everyday life. More than mere pastime, the "Circus" was a powerful political instrument, capable of shaping public opinion, exalting leaders, reinforcing cultural values, and, above all, distracting the population from government problems. While the people marveled at the bloody combats, athletic feats, and sumptuous ceremonies, complex political issues and administrative crises remained in the background, out of the focus of popular attention.

The distribution of "Bread" and the promotion of the "Circus" served clear political objectives. By guaranteeing food, the Roman government minimized popular dissatisfaction and reduced the likelihood of revolts. By offering free and large-scale entertainment, it diverted the people's interest from more delicate issues and channeled their emotions into the spectacle. This ingenious combination created a superficial sense of contentment, keeping the population under control and preserving the stability of the regime.

Although "Bread and Circuses" was a strategy of manipulation, it also reflected the complex relationship between power and people in Ancient Rome. Roman leaders understood that it was necessary to meet the basic needs of the population and provide mechanisms for social integration and emotional escape. The distribution of food and the organization of spectacles were, to some extent, a form of reward for loyalty and participation in the empire.

Even so, the effectiveness of this strategy as a tool of social control cannot be underestimated. Over the centuries, "Bread and Circuses" proved essential to maintaining order in Rome, even during periods of crisis. The rulers' ability to use food and entertainment as instruments of governance reveals a deep understanding of human psychology and social dynamics.

The legacy of this strategy has transcended the boundaries of classical antiquity. Although the forms of distraction and control have changed throughout history, the principle of "Bread and Circuses" remains surprisingly current. In different periods, governments and elites have adopted similar devices to divert public attention, maintain the status quo, and preserve their privileges.

The history of "Bread and Circuses" is not limited to an episode of Ancient Rome, but represents a recurring phenomenon that takes various forms over time. Comparing Ancient Rome with the modern world reveals the permanence of this distraction mechanism, adapted to new technologies and cultural habits. Today, the entertainment industry, professional sports, social media, and celebrity culture are sophisticated expansions of this concept.

If in Ancient Rome the "Circus" took place in physical arenas, today it is disseminated through TV screens, smartphones, and social networks, occupying all spaces of everyday life. "Bread," in turn, goes beyond the distribution of food, taking forms such as access to basic services and the promise of social ascension, even if often illusory.

The comparison between Rome and the current world shows that, despite cultural and technological transformations, the essence of the "Bread and Circuses" strategy remains intact. The manipulation of public attention, the diversion of focus from real problems, and the creation of artificial contentment continue to be powerful tools for those in power.

The perpetuation of this logic raises an essential question: to what extent are modern societies really aware of this cycle of distraction and control? Technology has exponentially expanded the reach of entertainment strategies, making them more subtle and sophisticated. The spectacle is no longer limited to physical arenas but infiltrates all aspects of daily life, shaping perceptions and priorities. While crowds turn to celebrity dramas, sports rivalries, and viral successes, fundamental issues about inequality, governance, and freedom remain on the margins of collective discussions.

Even so, history shows that, however effective distraction strategies may be, they are not infallible. At critical moments, when the empty promises of "Bread and Circuses" are no longer enough to contain dissatisfaction, the population awakens. Rome, despite its political ingenuity, did not resist its own contradictions and eventually collapsed under the weight of economic crises, corruption, and external invasions. The parallel with the present is inevitable: how long will modern societies be able to sustain a model that privileges spectacle instead of critical consciousness?

Looking to the future, the question is not whether "Bread and Circuses" will continue to exist, but how societies will react to it. Information is more accessible than ever, and those who challenge the logic of passivity find new forms of resistance and engagement. As long as there are those who question, analyze, and seek to understand the gears of power, there will always be the possibility of breaking with inertia and taking a more active role in shaping one's own destiny.

Chapter 3
The Brain and Emotion Addiction

The human brain functions as a complex learning and adaptation machine, shaped by millions of years of evolution to seek pleasure and avoid pain. Our emotions are not just fleeting responses to external stimuli, but an essential part of a sophisticated survival system. However, with the evolution of society and the departure from the natural conditions that shaped our biology, this same emotional mechanism has become vulnerable to excesses, leading to behavior patterns comparable to addiction. The incessant search for intense emotions – positive or negative – does not happen by chance; it is the result of the interaction between neurotransmitters, reward patterns, and the way the brain interprets the world around it. This dynamic, systematically exploited by entertainment and social structures, keeps individuals and crowds immersed in emotional cycles that can be as compulsive as any other type of addiction.

The brain's reward system, which motivates us to repeat pleasurable behaviors, is primarily guided by dopamine, a neurotransmitter fundamental to the sensation of pleasure and anticipation. Originally, this system reinforced behaviors essential for survival, such as eating, socializing, and reproducing. However, it can also be artificially stimulated by experiences that are not directly linked to our survival, but that provoke similar sensations of gratification and excitement. Sports, social media, politics, and entertainment operate as catalysts for these emotions, generating constant dopamine releases that encourage people to repeatedly return to these activities. The excitement of victory, the frustration of defeat, the frenzy of a controversy, or the excitement of a new trend function as emotional triggers that capture attention and create cycles of psychological dependence, leading many to prioritize these experiences over other areas of life.

As a consequence, the brain can become increasingly conditioned to seek intense emotions as the main source of stimulation, failing to value more subtle and lasting forms of well-being. Just as the excessive use of chemical substances alters the sensitivity of the reward system, constant exposure to strong emotional stimuli can cause a kind of desensitization, requiring increasingly larger doses of excitement to generate the same initial impact. This growing need for new emotions is reflected in the incessant search for entertainment, the obsession with sporting events, the constant checking of social media, and even the way we engage in ideological debates. To break this cycle, it is essential to understand its mechanisms and develop a more balanced relationship with emotions, allowing us to regain control over what truly provides us with meaning and genuine satisfaction.

Understanding emotion addiction requires delving into the functioning of the brain's reward system. Imagine an intricate neuronal circuit, composed of several interconnected brain areas, that is activated in response to stimuli considered beneficial or pleasurable. When we encounter something that the brain interprets as positive – a tasty food, a rewarding social interaction, or a personal achievement – this circuit is triggered, unleashing a cascade of neurochemical events that culminate in the release of neurotransmitters, chemical substances responsible for transmitting signals between neurons.

Among these neurotransmitters, dopamine stands out. Multifaceted and essential for brain function, it plays a crucial role in functions such as motor control, attention, motivation, and, especially, pleasure and reward. When dopamine is released, we experience sensations of euphoria, well-being, and satisfaction, which motivates us to repeat the behaviors that led to this release. It's as if the brain is saying, "This is good, do it again!"

In the context of "Bread and Circuses," neuroscience reveals why external events, such as sporting games and entertainment shows, exert such fascination over us. When someone watches a soccer game and gets excited about a goal, vibrating intensely with their team's victory, their brain receives a dopamine rush. The excitement, expectation, and sense of collective triumph function as powerful triggers for the reward system, flooding the brain with this neurotransmitter associated with pleasure. Repeated throughout life, this experience can create a pattern of seeking external emotional stimuli, turning into a vicious cycle.

Interestingly, the same reward system is also activated in the face of negative stimuli, albeit in a different way. When fans suffer from their team's defeat, frustration and disappointment activate areas of the brain linked to emotional pain, such as the anterior cingulate cortex and the amygdala. Although associated with suffering, these areas can also activate the reward system, as the brain seeks to alleviate the pain or understand the situation. In these moments, looking for explanations, finding culprits, or resorting to rituals of emotional catharsis are ways of trying to restore internal balance.

It is worth remembering that the reward system was not designed to make us addicted to soccer, celebrities, or social media. Its original function is to drive us to seek food, water, shelter, sexual partners, and cooperative social interactions, essential for survival and reproduction. However, the brain's ability to learn and adapt to experiences makes it susceptible to manipulation by repetitive and intense stimuli, even when these stimuli are not directly linked to our basic needs.

The entertainment industry has understood and exploited this brain vulnerability masterfully. Movies, series, games, music, and social media are strategically designed to activate the reward system, offering regular doses of emotional stimuli that keep the audience engaged and eager for more. The engaging narrative of a movie, the identification with charismatic characters, the emotion of a show, online social interaction, and competition in video games function as triggers for dopamine release, fueling a cycle of seeking pleasure and reward that can become compulsive.

Recent studies show that entertainment can cause behavioral addictions similar to those observed in gambling and problematic use of social media. Research indicates that people who spend excessive time consuming entertainment content can develop symptoms such as tolerance (need to increase the dose to get the same effect), withdrawal (discomfort when stopping access), loss of control (difficulty in limiting the time dedicated to entertainment), and impairment in other areas of life (problems in relationships, work, or studies).

The similarity between entertainment addiction and other behavioral addictions lies in the neurobiological mechanism behind both: the manipulation of the brain's reward system. Like drugs and gambling, entertainment can hijack reward circuits, leading to adaptations in the brain that increase its dependence on these stimuli. The incessant search for external emotions, driven by dopamine release, can become the focus of the individual's life, obscuring other sources of pleasure and more genuine and lasting satisfaction.

Breaking this cycle requires a conscious effort of rebalancing. Like any form of addiction, addiction to intense emotions can be mitigated through self-reflection and the adoption of healthier habits.

Developing the ability to appreciate moments of tranquility, investing in real interpersonal connections, and seeking less impulsive sources of satisfaction are fundamental steps in this process. Small changes, such as reducing exposure time to artificial stimuli, practicing mindfulness, and cultivating hobbies that provide pleasure in a balanced way, help reprogram the brain to value more subtle and lasting rewards.

This process, however, does not mean giving up emotions or denying their importance in the human experience. On the contrary, it is about rescuing the authenticity of our emotional responses, allowing them to be fully lived, without the need for exaggerated and incessant stimuli. True emotional freedom is not in the unbridled pursuit of pleasure or in the flight from pain, but in the ability to navigate between different emotional states with awareness and balance. Only then is it possible to escape the trap of a mind constantly hostage to its own compulsions.

By understanding the mechanisms that underpin emotion addiction, we can transform the way we interact with the world around us. Instead of remaining passive in the face of strategies that exploit our biology to keep us engaged and consuming, we can take control of our experiences and choices. Ultimately, the key to a healthier emotional life is not to eliminate intense emotions, but to learn to dose them, appreciating both the fervor of a great moment and the serenity of the little things in everyday life.

Chapter 4
Psychology of the Crowd

The presence in a crowd provokes subtle, yet profound, transformations in human behavior. The individual, previously guided by their personal identity and values, becomes integrated into a collective organism, where emotions, impulses, and decisions operate under a new logic. The psychology of the crowd seeks to understand this change, analyzing how large groups shape perceptions, influence judgments, and intensify emotional reactions. The fascination with collective events – from sporting celebrations to political demonstrations – reveals the strength of this dynamic, in which the feeling of belonging and shared energy create intense and often unpredictable experiences. The crowd is not just a collection of people; it is a psychological phenomenon capable of diluting individual identities, amplifying emotions, and generating behaviors that, in isolation, would be improbable or even unthinkable.

The anonymity provided by the mass favors the so-called deindividuation, a psychological state in which self-awareness and personal responsibility decrease. This phenomenon explains why peaceful people can become aggressive in protests, rational fans can react violently to a game, and audiences can engage in behaviors they would normally avoid. The reduction of individual inhibition, coupled with emotional contagion – the rapid spread of feelings and reactions among participants – makes the crowd a highly suggestible environment. Emotions intensify in a cascade effect: a small group starting an enthusiastic demonstration can, in minutes, infect thousands, transforming a peaceful environment into a stage of collective euphoria or fury. This phenomenon, far from being random, is exploited in various contexts, from political campaigns that inflame passions to marketing strategies that stimulate mass emotional reactions.

The crowd's vulnerability to external influence creates fertile ground for charismatic leaders, inflammatory speeches, and symbols that evoke immediate emotional responses. The crowd does not analyze coldly; it reacts, feels, and responds instinctively. Slogans, anthems, flags, and synchronized gestures reinforce group cohesion and reduce individual critical thinking. This fusion of identities can both inspire acts of solidarity and trigger outbursts of violence. Understanding the mechanisms of crowd psychology is essential for navigating a world where digital and physical masses are constantly mobilized for different purposes. The challenge is to balance the desire for belonging with critical awareness, channeling collective energy constructively, without compromising individual autonomy and discernment.

Social psychology, over decades of research, has shown that human behavior is profoundly influenced by the social context. When we are in groups, our actions, thoughts, and emotions tend to deviate from individual patterns, aligning with collective norms. In the crowd, this influence intensifies exponentially, giving rise to unique and often surprising behavioral phenomena.

One of the pillars of crowd psychology is the idea that individual identity dissolves into the group. The anonymity generated by the mass diminishes self-awareness and personal responsibility. The individual, immersed in the crowd, feels less exposed to judgment, which can reduce inhibitions and increase impulsivity. This process, known as deindividuation, does not necessarily mean destructive behaviors, but it favors actions that, in isolation, would be atypical or extreme.

The temporary loss of personal identity is linked to emotional contagion. In large groups, emotions spread rapidly, like waves sweeping across the mass. Laughter, crying, anger, and enthusiasm spread among individuals, amplifying in the process. This contagion is facilitated by unconscious imitation, a basic psychological mechanism that leads us to mirror the facial expressions, body posture, and tone of voice of those around us. In the crowd, this imitation becomes massive, creating a collective emotional state that dominates the individual experience.

Gustave Le Bon, one of the pioneers in the study of crowd psychology, described the crowd as a distinct psychological entity, endowed with its own characteristics, which transcend the sum of the individualities that compose it. In his work *Psychologie des Foules* (1895), he argued that the crowd is irrational, impulsive, and suggestible. For him, individuals, upon merging into the mass, lose the ability for critical and rational thinking, being dominated by primitive impulses and basic emotions. Although his view is considered pessimistic and generalizing, his ideas laid the foundation for the study of this complex phenomenon.

Studies on the mass effect show that sporting events, political demonstrations, and musical shows are environments conducive to the intensification of collective emotional reactions. In football stadiums, club passion, fueled by rivalries and group identity, finds a stage to manifest itself intensely. The victory of the favorite team generates explosions of joy and unison chants, while defeat can result in frustration, anger, and even violence. In political demonstrations, ideological fervor can lead to passionate behaviors, from peaceful protests to confrontations. In concerts, the communion around an artist or musical genre creates an atmosphere of euphoria, amplified by music, dance, and social interaction.

The temporary loss of personal identity, combined with emotional contagion and the decrease in individual responsibility, facilitates emotional manipulation. Charismatic leaders and skilled orators exploit these dynamics to influence opinions, incite passions, and direct behaviors. In mass events, people tend to follow the group's opinion without rational questioning, accept suggestions without critical analysis, and act on momentary impulses. This susceptibility to emotional manipulation is one of the most worrying aspects of crowd psychology, especially in a world where information and disinformation compete for public attention.

The psychological malleability of the crowd can be used for both good and evil. Positive social movements show how collective cohesion generates significant changes, inspiring solidarity and joint action for noble causes. However, the same force that unites can also blind, making individuals vulnerable to manipulative speeches and disproportionate reactions. When emotion overrides reason, discernment is lost, and the collective can be driven by impulses that would hardly be accepted individually.

The digital age has amplified this phenomenon, transforming physical crowds into virtual masses, where anonymity and emotional contagion operate with even greater intensity. Social networks function as modern arenas, where opinions spread rapidly, conflicts flare up, and movements gain strength in a matter of hours. The same mechanism that, in the past, led crowds to acclaim charismatic leaders or start riots in the streets now manifests itself through likes, shares, and heated comments. The difference is that, in the digital environment, the speed of propagation and the lack of physical contact intensify polarization, creating collective thought bubbles that reinforce extreme beliefs and emotions.

In this scenario, critical awareness becomes essential. Understanding the mechanisms of crowd psychology does not mean rejecting the feeling of belonging, but learning to balance it with autonomy and reflection. Collective energy can be a powerful tool, as long as it is guided by discernment and responsibility. By recognizing how emotions are amplified in the collective and how external influences shape behaviors, it becomes possible to participate in groups without losing individuality. After all, being among many does not mean ceasing to be oneself.

Chapter 5
The Impact on Individual Identity

Individual identity is a dynamic construction, shaped throughout life by experiences, values, choices, and social interactions. Essentially, it represents the perception we have of ourselves, influenced by both internal and external factors. However, in a hyperconnected society, where external stimuli constantly compete for our attention, maintaining a solid and authentic identity becomes an increasing challenge. Many, without realizing it, shift the source of their self-esteem and sense of worth outside of themselves, tying their identity to achievements, ideologies, or external figures. This phenomenon, known as identity transfer, can compromise personal development, making self-esteem vulnerable to factors beyond individual control.

Emotional dependence on external elements can manifest in various ways. Passionate sports fans may feel that their lives gain meaning through the victories of a team. Celebrity admirers can build their self-image based on identification with public figures, assimilating their achievements as if they were their own. In ideological contexts, followers of certain movements may lose the ability to critically analyze by completely merging with the cause they defend, interpreting any criticism as an attack on their own identity. In these cases, individuality dissolves, and emotional well-being becomes dependent on the success or failure of these external entities. This not only weakens self-esteem, making it unstable and reactive, but it can also lead to frustration, a sense of powerlessness, and a distorted view of one's own life.

Rebuilding a strong and balanced identity requires reflection and internal realignment. It is necessary to refocus on self-knowledge, valuing one's own achievements and investing in the development of genuine skills and purposes. Strengthening identity involves accepting vulnerabilities and limitations without leading to self-deprecation. Seeking sources of satisfaction and fulfillment based on personal effort, rather than unpredictable external events, allows for the construction of a more stable and resilient self-esteem. By understanding the mechanisms of identity transfer and its consequences, it is possible to adopt a more conscious and autonomous stance towards the world, cultivating an identity that does not depend on external circumstances but truly reflects who one is.

In a world saturated with external stimuli, the temptation to define one's own worth based on the accomplishments of others becomes particularly strong. Many people, albeit unconsciously, try to fill an inner void or compensate for low self-esteem by projecting their aspirations onto sports teams, celebrities, political figures, or social movements. By becoming fervent supporters of a football club, for example, they can internalize the team's victories and defeats as if they were their own, attributing to themselves a sense of value and belonging derived from the team's performance. Similarly, idolatry of a public figure can lead to excessive identification with their achievements and trajectory, shaping self-image and personal aspirations based on an external and, often, unattainable model.

This phenomenon occurs when the individual shifts the center of their self-assessment outward, anchoring their self-esteem and sense of worth in achievements and attributes that do not directly belong to them. Instead of cultivating internal qualities, developing personal skills, and pursuing authentic goals, they begin to define their worth based on the performance of a team, the success of a celebrity, or the rise of an ideological movement. Thus, happiness and self-esteem become hostage to external and uncontrollable events, subject to unpredictable fluctuations.

The psychological damage of this identity transfer can be profound. First, self-esteem becomes unstable and vulnerable, fluctuating according to the performance of the idolized external entity. Victories and successes can generate euphoria and self-satisfaction, while defeats and failures can plunge the individual into frustration and devaluation. This emotional roller coaster, driven by external factors, can generate anxiety, irritability, and a chronic sense of instability.

Furthermore, this dependence can impair the ability to deal with personal failures and challenges. When self-esteem is anchored in the achievements of others, any personal setback becomes even more difficult to bear. If self-worth depends on success, failure can be interpreted as proof of incompetence or lack of value. This difficulty in dealing with losses can lead to a fear of taking risks, avoidance of challenges, and a cycle of self-sabotage, in which the individual prevents themselves from pursuing their own goals and exploring their potential.

Constant comparison with idealized external models, such as celebrities and public figures, also contributes to the erosion of self-esteem and the weakening of individual identity. Media and social networks display idealized and often unreal versions of life, promoting standards of beauty, success, and happiness unattainable for most. Continuous exposure to these narratives can generate feelings of inadequacy, envy, and self-criticism, eroding self-confidence and hindering the acceptance of one's own individuality.

Emotional dependence on external events, fueled by identity transfer, can lead to neglect of one's own life, interpersonal relationships, and personal growth. People excessively involved with organized fan groups, fan clubs, or extreme ideological movements may dedicate a disproportionate amount of their time and energy to these activities, neglecting studies, work, family, and friends. Over time, personal life begins to revolve around these external passions, which, although intense, do not contribute to individual development or the fulfillment of authentic purposes.

To avoid the damages of identity transfer, it is essential to turn attention inward, cultivating personal qualities, developing skills, and pursuing one's own goals. Valuing individual achievements, recognizing the uniqueness of one's own trajectory, and building a solid and resilient self-esteem, based on internal values and not on external validation, are essential steps. Strengthening identity involves accepting one's own imperfections, recognizing one's talents, and seeking a life purpose aligned with one's deepest values and aspirations.

Rebuilding a solid identity is an ongoing process of reflection and self-knowledge. This does not mean abandoning passions, but understanding that they cannot be the sole basis of self-esteem and personal sense of worth. True emotional security arises from learning to celebrate external victories without them defining who you are and facing failures without them shaking your own essence. Only by developing this emotional independence is it possible to balance involvement with the external world and the cultivation of an authentic identity.

Furthermore, taking ownership of one's own life requires a new way of dealing with challenges and frustrations. Instead of seeking validation in external figures or the achievements of others, it is essential to set personal goals and value small individual advances. Real growth happens when motivation comes from within, not from the need to mirror idealized models. This process, although challenging, strengthens emotional resilience and allows for a more fulfilling life, guided by genuine choices, not by unconscious emotional dependencies.

Ultimately, building a strong and balanced identity involves recognizing one's own individuality amidst the whirlwind of external influences. Identity does not need to be a response to the world, but an authentic expression of who one is. By rediscovering one's own worth, independent of external factors, a healthier relationship with the world is created, where passions and interests cease to be emotional anchors and become part of the journey of self-discovery and growth.

Chapter 6
The Power of Narratives

Narratives play a central role in human experience, being one of the most powerful means of communication, learning, and transmission of values throughout history. Since the earliest civilizations, myths and tales have been used to explain natural phenomena, establish social norms, and strengthen the collective identity of peoples and communities. More than simple accounts, stories shape the perception of the world and profoundly influence emotions, beliefs, and behaviors. In the contemporary scenario, where media and entertainment exert a predominant influence on daily life, narratives have evolved to become sophisticated tools of emotional engagement and persuasion. With advanced storytelling techniques, the information and entertainment industry creates engaging stories that capture the public's attention, arouse intense reactions, and foster deep identifications. This phenomenon directly impacts the way people interpret reality and interact with the world around them.

The ability of narratives to generate immersion and emotional identification is not only a reflection of human creativity, but also a widely studied mechanism of social and psychological influence. When a story is well constructed, it activates areas of the brain responsible for emotional processing and empathy, making the audience feel part of the narrated experience. This connection can be so intense that, often, the line between fiction and reality becomes blurred. Whether through books, movies, series, political speeches, or sporting events, stories promote a sense of belonging and meaning that can be highly mobilizing. However, this same force that allows narratives to inspire, educate, and entertain can also be used to manipulate, diverting the public's attention from essential issues and reinforcing limiting beliefs or artificial polarizations. The deliberate use of emotional narratives to influence behaviors and opinions is one of the most effective strategies of mass communication, ensuring continuous engagement and audience loyalty.

Given the omnipresence of narratives in contemporary society, it is essential to develop a critical eye on the discourses and stories we consume daily. By recognizing the narrative techniques used to arouse emotions and create identification, it is possible to differentiate stories that broaden the perception of the world from those that only reinforce pre-established patterns of thought and behavior. Understanding the power of narratives does not mean rejecting them, but rather interpreting them consciously, avoiding being led by discourses that serve external interests. In this way, it is possible not only to appreciate good stories, but also to use the knowledge about storytelling to create our own narratives, based on authenticity, reflection, and autonomy.

The essence of a narrative lies in its ability to transport us to another time, another place, another perspective. Good stories involve us, make us feel part of the plot, connect us emotionally to the characters, and lead us to experience, albeit indirectly, their joys, sorrows, challenges, and triumphs. This immersion and identification are fundamental pillars of the power of narratives. By recognizing ourselves in fictional characters and situations, we project our own emotions and aspirations onto their journeys, experiencing a sense of emotional participation that can be deeply engaging.

Media and entertainment understand this dynamic and exploit it systematically. Whether on television, in sports, in cinema, in games, or on social media, there is a deliberate effort to transform events and public figures into captivating narratives, capable of arousing deep feelings and ensuring continuous engagement. This strategy of constructing emotional narratives is one of the main mechanisms for maintaining the phenomenon of "Bread and Circuses" today.

One of the most effective techniques in this construction is the creation of heroes and villains. Engaging stories are generally structured around archetypal characters who represent opposing forces, personifying good and evil, virtue and vice, success and failure. In sports, this is evident in the construction of rivalries between teams and athletes, transforming competitions into epic duels. In politics, public debate often relies on polarized narratives, where leaders and parties are portrayed as saviors or threats. In cinema and television, the figure of the righteous hero and the cruel villain are recurring archetypes that resonate with the public, arousing emotions of admiration, repudiation, hope, and fear.

Another powerful tool in building captivating narratives is emotional polarization. By presenting situations and characters as irreconcilable opposites, media and entertainment intensify the public's emotional engagement. Polarization stimulates identification with one side of the narrative and rejection of the other, creating a sense of belonging and opposition that is extremely mobilizing. In the political context, this divides society into opposing camps, fueling rivalries and conflicts that divert attention from more complex issues. In sports, the rivalry between fans and clubs is exploited to the fullest, ensuring loyalty and audience.

Emotional narratives, by arousing intense feelings of joy, sadness, anger, fear, hope, and belonging, can generate a strong sense of identification and engagement. When we are moved by the victory of a team, the journey of a fictional hero, or the fiery speech of a political leader, we feel as if we are actively participating in that story, as if our emotions and support were decisive in the unfolding of events. This illusion of participation is one of the psychological mechanisms that keep the public emotionally involved, keeping them away from more relevant issues that really impact their lives.

The constant repetition of emotional narratives in media and entertainment can create a cycle of dependence, in which the individual increasingly seeks external stimuli to fill an inner void or make up for a lack of purpose. The incessant search for intense emotions, through the consumption of engaging stories, can become a form of escapism, a way to avoid confronting personal challenges and existential questions. This emotional dependence on external narratives can obscure the need to build our own life stories, based on our values, goals, and authentic experiences.

Recognizing how narratives influence our emotions and perceptions does not mean rejecting them, but using them consciously. Understanding how they shape our worldview makes us more critical consumers and more responsible narrators. Instead of just absorbing ready-made discourses, we begin to question them, identifying their intentions, effects, and the impact they have on our beliefs and decisions. Thus, we avoid falling into the trap of manipulation and alienation, transforming the narrative experience into an instrument of learning and reflection.

More than just passively receiving the stories we are told, we have the chance to create and share our own. Each person carries a unique trajectory, full of challenges, discoveries, and transformations, and giving voice to this experience is a powerful way to exercise autonomy and meaning. When we become protagonists of our own narratives, we stop depending on the plots imposed on us and start building authentic stories, aligned with our truths and purposes.

The true power of narratives lies not only in their ability to move and engage, but also in the possibility of liberation and self-knowledge they offer. Instead of getting lost in other people's stories, we can use this understanding to give meaning to our own journey, writing a plot that reflects our values and aspirations and inspires others to do the same.

Chapter 7
The Political Use of Emotion

Politics has always been deeply connected to human emotions, as it is through them that bonds of belonging, mobilization, and collective engagement are built. Since the dawn of civilizations, rulers and leaders have understood that controlling the emotions of the masses is a powerful tool for consolidating authority and maintaining dominance over society. Fear, hope, anger, and patriotism are some of the emotions frequently exploited to direct behaviors and shape perceptions. In the contemporary scenario, this dynamic not only persists but becomes even more sophisticated with advances in communication technologies and media strategies. Emotions are manipulated to amplify narratives, direct debates, and influence political decisions, making the public sphere an environment increasingly susceptible to impulsive reactions and sharp polarizations.

When used strategically, emotion transforms politics into a spectacle, where rational arguments give way to fiery speeches, striking symbols, and Manichean narratives. The advent of social media and mass media outlets has enhanced this phenomenon, allowing emotionally charged messages to spread with impressive speed. Election campaigns, for example, are not only based on concrete proposals but, above all, on impactful slogans, emblematic images, and speeches that awaken deep feelings in voters. This strategy not only captures the public's attention but also keeps them in continuous cycles of outrage, hope, or fear, making them more susceptible to manipulation and less prone to critical and thoughtful analysis of the facts. Emotional engagement surpasses reason, making politics increasingly resemble entertainment, where spectacle overrides content and immediate reaction replaces in-depth reflection.

Extreme polarization, one of the most striking effects of the political exploitation of emotions, fuels rivalries and makes constructive dialogue between different perspectives impossible. When politics becomes an emotional battlefield, people stop evaluating arguments objectively and start reacting viscerally, reinforcing their beliefs and rejecting any opposing view. This scenario benefits leaders who exploit social division to consolidate power, while weakening society's ability to debate and solve problems effectively. To resist this dynamic, it is essential to develop critical thinking capable of identifying and questioning the emotional strategies used in politics, promoting a more conscious and informed stance in the face of the narratives that surround us.

Just as the entertainment industry masters the art of constructing emotional narratives to captivate the public, contemporary politics uses the same techniques to engage voters, mobilize activists, and shape public opinion. The line that separated the spectacle from the seriousness of politics has become increasingly blurred, giving way to a hybrid scenario where emotion is the main currency. Political campaigns, leaders' speeches, public debates, and even media coverage of political events often resemble entertainment shows, prioritizing emotional impact over rational argumentation and thoughtful debate.

One of the most effective mechanisms of emotional manipulation in politics is the exploitation of fanaticism and polarization. Fanaticism, by definition, is a blind and irrational adherence to a cause, ideology, or leadership, marked by intolerance to criticism, passionate exaltation, and the willingness to defend one's idols at any cost. Politics, like sports and religion, offers fertile ground for fanaticism, especially when leaders and parties use group identities, historical rivalries, and collective fears to strengthen their support and create a sense of exclusive belonging.

Polarization works by dividing society into opposing and irreconcilable camps, intensifying rivalries and fueling conflicts. In the political arena, this strategy manifests itself in the radical opposition between ideologies, parties, and social groups, creating an environment of animosity and distrust. Leaders and parties often resort to polarization to strengthen their base, demonizing opponents and presenting themselves as the only possible solution for the country. Although efficient in mobilizing voters and consolidating power, this approach weakens public debate, hinders the search for consensual solutions, and threatens social cohesion.

The similarity between political fervor and sports fanaticism is remarkable. In both cases, blind passion obscures reason, criticism, and objectivity. Fanatical fans defend their teams with the same vehemence and intolerance with which ideological militants defend their political beliefs. The defeat of a team or the rise of an opposing party are experienced as personal tragedies, generating passionate reactions that often exceed the limits of civility and common sense. This equivalence between sports and political fanaticism highlights the emotional nature of adherence to groups and ideologies, whether they are linked to sports or politics.

Historical and contemporary examples of this phenomenon are abundant. Totalitarian regimes of the 20th century, such as Nazism and Fascism, exploited ideological fanaticism and the cult of personality to mobilize the masses and consolidate power. Propaganda campaigns, grandiose parades, fiery speeches, and the demonization of minorities were used to create a state of collective hysteria and patriotic fervor, suppressing opposition and silencing critical voices. In today's world, the growth of populism and political extremism in various parts of the world also feeds on the exploitation of primary emotions, such as fear, anger, and resentment, creating a climate of polarization and intolerance that threatens democracy and peaceful coexistence.

Contemporary political campaigns are meticulously structured to activate intense emotions in voters, using marketing, propaganda, and persuasive communication techniques similar to those of the entertainment industry. Opinion polls, focus groups, and data analysis help identify the issues and messages that most resonate with the public, exploiting their fears, desires, and aspirations. Speeches, election advertisements, televised debates, and social media posts are carefully crafted to generate emotional impact, with emotive language, striking images, music, and slogans that appeal to feelings, leaving reason in the background.

The exhaustive repetition of simplistic and polarized messages, the personification of politics around charismatic figures, and the creation of Manichean narratives are common strategies in election campaigns. The goal is to generate commotion and emotional engagement, preventing people from rationally analyzing the facts, proposals, and arguments. Instead of voting based on the evaluation of government programs and candidates' competencies, many voters are guided by emotions, identification with leaders, or aversion to opponents.

The political use of emotion is not limited to election periods. Rulers and parties continuously resort to emotional manipulation strategies to maintain popular support, divert attention from urgent problems, and neutralize criticism and opposition. Choreographed events, controversial statements, rhetorical attacks, and the dissemination of disinformation are tools to keep the population in a constant state of commotion and emotional engagement, hindering critical reflection and qualified debate.

Faced with this scenario, it is essential to adopt a critical and reflective stance so as not to be mere spectators of this emotional spectacle, but rather conscious agents in the political debate. Emotion, when properly directed, can drive positive social transformations, but when manipulated, it becomes an instrument of control and alienation. Identifying the strategies used to capture and direct feelings allows each individual to make more informed political decisions, based not only on what resonates emotionally but also on principles, values, and a rational analysis of the facts.

The challenge is to balance emotion and reason in political involvement. Outrage at injustice and hope for a better future are legitimate fuels for social action, but it is necessary to prevent these feelings from being exploited to transform us into pieces of a power game. Politics cannot be reduced to inflamed passions or blind rivalries, as real change happens through dialogue, negotiation, and the collective construction of solutions. The more we understand the emotional mechanisms at play, the less we will be manipulated by speeches loaded with fear or hate and the more we will be able to exercise our citizenship responsibly.

Political emancipation, therefore, depends on the ability to see beyond the emotional narratives presented to us, developing a broader and more questioning perspective. When we cease to be merely reactive and become conscious participants in the political process, we break the cycle of manipulation and open space for a more authentic and constructive debate. Thus, politics can once again be a field of genuine reflection and transformation, instead of a spectacle where emotions are exploited to consolidate power and perpetuate artificial divisions.

Chapter 8
The Herd Effect

The human tendency to follow the behavior of the majority, often without rational questioning, is deeply rooted in social psychology and significantly influences our individual and collective decisions. The herd effect occurs when individuals adopt beliefs or behaviors simply because they observe other people doing the same, without necessarily understanding the reasons behind those actions. This phenomenon, widely studied in areas such as economics and sociology, is not only a reflection of the survival instinct but also a mechanism of social adaptation that can both facilitate cooperation and lead to irrational and dangerous choices. The desire for belonging and the aversion to social isolation lead people to align their attitudes with those of the group, generating patterns of collective behavior that vary in intensity and impact, depending on the context.

The influence of the herd effect is especially visible in moments of uncertainty or crisis, when people seek security in social validation. Faced with ambiguous situations, with limited or contradictory information, the natural tendency is to observe others to decide how to act. This mechanism can be useful when collective behavior is based on well-informed decisions, but it can also generate negative consequences when the group is guided by emotional impulses or incorrect information. In the financial market, for example, the herd effect can fuel speculative bubbles or sharp drops, as investors buy or sell assets just because others are doing the same. In crises, such as natural disasters or collective panics, following the crowd without critical evaluation can result in hasty and, in some cases, harmful decisions for individual and collective safety.

Although the herd effect is an inevitable phenomenon of life in society, it is essential to balance the need for belonging with the capacity for critical thinking. Questioning behavior patterns, seeking diverse sources of information, and exercising intellectual autonomy are fundamental attitudes to avoid the risks of blind conformity. Strengthening education, social awareness, and individual responsibility helps reduce vulnerability to external influences and ensures that choices are made based on reflection and knowledge, not just imitation of the behavior of others. Understanding the herd effect allows us to see beyond group dynamics and act with more discernment in a world where information and collective influence play an increasingly central role.

At the heart of the herd effect is the human need for social acceptance, a drive intrinsic to our nature. Since the dawn of humanity, survival has depended on cohesion and cooperation within groups. Isolated individuals faced greater difficulties in finding resources and protection, becoming easy prey. Thus, the ability to integrate, conform to social norms, and be accepted by the community became an essential evolutionary advantage. This innate predisposition to social conformity, shaped by millions of years of evolution, still echoes in our current behavior, leading us to seek approval and avoid isolation or rejection.

The herd effect occurs when this need for social acceptance overrides individual critical thinking. In contexts of uncertainty, ambiguity, or social pressure, people tend to observe and imitate the behavior of others to guide their own actions. If a large number of individuals adopt a certain belief, behavior, or emotion, others may feel compelled to follow them, even without fully understanding the reasons behind this collective choice. This adherence to the behavior of the majority can be conscious or unconscious, driven by the desire to fit in, avoid ostracism, and feel part of the group.

The influence of the herd effect is particularly strong in ambiguous or complex social scenarios, where information is scarce or contradictory. In moments of crisis, panic, or collective euphoria, individual rationality can be quickly suppressed by group pressure, leading to impulsive and irrational behaviors. In the financial market, for example, this phenomenon can intensify speculative bubbles and economic crises, with investors acting hastily, driven by the fear of missing opportunities or by collective hysteria. In emergency situations, such as fires or natural disasters, the herd effect can trigger disorderly and dangerous escapes, with individuals following the crowd without rationally evaluating the best escape routes or safety strategies.

The herd effect also influences fads, cultural trends, and social movements. When a product, style of dress, music, or idea gains popularity, this trend can amplify rapidly, leading to massive adherence, often without critical reflection. In organized fan groups, for example, this phenomenon manifests itself in the standardization of behaviors, chants, and emotional reactions, reinforcing a strong sense of group identity. In protests and political demonstrations, participation can be driven by the emotional involvement of the group, leading initially hesitant individuals to engage due to the massive adherence of other people. In the cultural and social sphere, the herd effect can accelerate changes and transformations, expanding the influence of ideas and values.

It is important to recognize that, although it can lead to irrational and impulsive behaviors, the herd effect also has an adaptive function. In complex social environments, following the majority can be an efficient strategy to save time and energy in decision-making. When information is limited or time is short, relying on collective judgment can be more practical than conducting a detailed individual analysis. Furthermore, the herd effect can strengthen social cohesion, promote cooperation, and facilitate the coordination of actions in groups, essential factors for the survival and success of human communities.

However, excessive dependence on the herd effect can lead to the loss of individuality, the suppression of critical thinking, and vulnerability to social manipulation. Individuals who follow the crowd without reflection become more susceptible to unfounded beliefs, rumors, disinformation, and propaganda. Leaders and interest groups can exploit this phenomenon to manipulate public opinion, direct collective behaviors, and consolidate power. The dissemination of fake news and distorted information on social networks, for example, often benefits from this mechanism, as content is shared without verification, driven by the belief that popularity indicates credibility.

Developing a critical awareness of the herd effect is essential to balance the need for belonging with intellectual autonomy. Questioning trends, analyzing information independently, and resisting social pressure are fundamental skills to prevent the search for acceptance from leading us to thoughtless choices. In a world where the speed of information often surpasses its veracity, knowing how to differentiate impulsive adherence from conscious decision becomes a crucial differentiator to preserve the integrity of individual thought.

Furthermore, recognizing our natural inclination to follow the majority allows this phenomenon to be used constructively. The same effect that can spread disinformation or stimulate irrational behaviors can also be directed to drive positive social changes. When critical and informed individuals influence groups with ethics and transparency, waves of transformation are created based on reason and cooperation, instead of mere emotional contagion. Thus, collective awareness is strengthened without sacrificing individuality.

In the end, dealing with the herd effect does not mean rejecting it completely, but understanding its mechanisms and learning to navigate them with discernment. Instead of automatically reacting to what the majority does, we can become attentive observers and active participants in society, balancing instinct and reflection. In this way, we transform the impulse to follow the group into a deliberate and conscious choice, ensuring that our actions express not only the desire for belonging but also genuine values and convictions.

Capítulo 9
As Redes Sociais e a Nova Arena

A ascensão das redes sociais foi uma das transformações mais profundas da era digital, mudando a forma como as pessoas se comunicam, consomem informações e interagem com o mundo. Antes, a comunicação de massa era centralizada em veículos tradicionais como jornais, rádio e televisão. Com a internet, esse processo se descentralizou, permitindo que qualquer indivíduo se tornasse emissor de conteúdo. No entanto, essa democratização da informação trouxe desafios significativos, transformando as redes sociais não apenas em ferramentas de conexão, mas também em arenas de disputa por atenção, onde a lógica do engajamento se sobrepõe à do conhecimento. A velocidade com que as informações circulam, somada aos algoritmos que favorecem conteúdos carregados de emoção, criou um ambiente onde indignação, entretenimento efêmero e polarização são amplificados, afastando a atenção de debates mais profundos e reflexivos.

O design dessas plataformas não é acidental, mas pensado para maximizar o tempo de permanência dos usuários e estimular interações constantes. Os algoritmos priorizam conteúdos que despertam reações intensas, sejam positivas ou negativas. Quanto mais engajamento um conteúdo gera — na forma de curtidas, comentários ou compartilhamentos —, maior sua visibilidade. Isso significa que publicações que exploram emoções fortes, como medo, raiva ou euforia, se espalham rapidamente, enquanto informações mais equilibradas e reflexivas tendem a ficar em segundo plano. Esse mecanismo cria ciclos viciantes de consumo de conteúdo, incentivando reações impulsivas, muitas vezes sem verificação da veracidade das informações ou ponderação sobre suas implicações. Assim, as redes sociais se tornam não apenas veículos de comunicação, mas também instrumentos de manipulação emocional, influenciando percepções e comportamentos de maneira sutil e contínua.

Essa nova dinâmica digital reforça a lógica do espetáculo e do entretenimento, lembrando o conceito de "Pão e Circo" da Roma Antiga. Se no passado os grandes coliseus serviam para distrair a população, hoje as redes sociais cumprem esse papel, oferecendo um fluxo incessante de conteúdos que capturam a atenção e desviam o foco de questões mais relevantes. Discussões acaloradas sobre temas triviais, polêmicas fabricadas e a constante busca por validação social substituem debates substanciais, fragmentando o discurso público. Para escapar dessa armadilha, é essencial desenvolver uma relação mais consciente com essas plataformas, questionando seus mecanismos e buscando formas de consumo de informação que priorizem reflexão crítica e conhecimento verdadeiro, em vez de simples reações emocionais imediatas.

Compreender o impacto das redes sociais no contexto do "Pão e Circo" exige analisar seu funcionamento e a maneira como moldam nossa experiência online. Essas plataformas são, essencialmente, espaços virtuais de interação, onde indivíduos podem se conectar, compartilhar informações, expressar opiniões, construir comunidades e participar de debates públicos. A conectividade global e instantânea, aliada à facilidade de produção e disseminação de conteúdo, deu às redes sociais um poder de influência sem precedentes na sociedade contemporânea.

Entretanto, a aparente democratização da informação e a promessa de conexão social coexistem com mecanismos que podem acentuar distração, polarização e manipulação emocional. Buscando engajamento e receita publicitária, as plataformas utilizam algoritmos que priorizam conteúdos que geram reações extremas. Essa lógica, diretamente ligada ao modelo de negócios das redes sociais, cria um ciclo vicioso de busca por atenção, em que conteúdos sensacionalistas, polêmicos e carregados de emoção tendem a se destacar e viralizar, enquanto informações mais relevantes, debates ponderados e conteúdos mais densos acabam relegados a segundo plano.

As redes sociais, nesse sentido, tornaram-se verdadeiras arenas digitais, onde a atenção é a moeda mais valiosa e a competição por ela é implacável. Assim como o Coliseu romano reunia multidões para espetáculos sangrentos e emocionantes, as redes sociais atraem bilhões de usuários diariamente, oferecendo um fluxo contínuo de estímulos sensoriais e emocionais que competem ferozmente por atenção. Nessa nova arena digital, a lógica do espetáculo e do entretenimento se intensifica, e a busca por emoções instantâneas e gratificação imediata muitas vezes se sobrepõe à busca por informação relevante, conhecimento aprofundado e reflexão crítica.

O design dessas plataformas e sua dinâmica algorítmica criam ciclos de engajamento emocional intensos e persistentes. No Twitter, por exemplo, a efemeridade das mensagens e a velocidade do fluxo de informações incentivam debates acalorados, discussões polarizadas e reações impulsivas a eventos e notícias. O Facebook, com seu foco em conexões pessoais e grupos temáticos, amplifica o compartilhamento de opiniões e emoções dentro de círculos sociais homogêneos, reforçando o viés de confirmação e a polarização ideológica. O Instagram, com sua ênfase em imagens e vídeos curtos e impactantes, explora o apelo visual e a gratificação instantânea, criando um ambiente propício à comparação social, à busca por validação externa e à disseminação de estilos de vida idealizados e muitas vezes irreais. O TikTok, com seus vídeos curtos e virais, impulsionados por algoritmos altamente personalizados, intensifica o consumo de entretenimento rápido e superficial, gerando um ciclo vicioso de distração constante.

Nesses ciclos de engajamento emocional, as pessoas frequentemente se envolvem em discussões acaloradas e reações passionais a eventos e notícias que, muitas vezes, não compreendem totalmente ou que não afetam diretamente suas vidas. A velocidade do fluxo de informações, a superficialidade dos conteúdos e a pressão social para participar de debates e expressar opiniões contribuem para ciclos de comoção coletiva e indignação moral, que se espalham rapidamente pelas redes, consumindo tempo, energia e atenção em detrimento de questões mais relevantes.

    Os algoritmos, ao priorizarem conteúdos que geram reações extremas, desempenham um papel crucial na amplificação do fenômeno do "Pão e Circo" nas redes sociais. Buscando maximizar o engajamento e o tempo de permanência dos usuários, esses sistemas favorecem conteúdos que despertam emoções intensas, sejam elas positivas ou negativas. Notícias sensacionalistas, manchetes alarmistas, vídeos chocantes, discursos inflamados e conteúdos polarizados ganham destaque e viralizam porque geram mais cliques, curtidas e compartilhamentos do que conteúdos mais equilibrados e informativos. Essa lógica algorítmica cria um ambiente informacional distorcido, em que a busca por atenção e engajamento emocional se sobrepõe à busca por informação precisa, análise crítica e debate racional.

    As redes sociais, ao se tornarem a nova arena da distração e da manipulação emocional, desviam a atenção de questões mais importantes que impactam a sociedade. Enquanto usuários se envolvem em debates sobre temas triviais, fofocas de celebridades e polêmicas passageiras, questões como desigualdade social, mudanças climáticas, crises políticas, problemas de saúde pública e desafios econômicos são frequentemente deixados de lado. Essa distração massiva, impulsionada pela lógica algorítmica e pela busca incessante por engajamento emocional, perpetua o ciclo do "Pão e Circo" contemporâneo, mantendo a população entretida e distraída, enquanto temas mais urgentes permanecem sem solução.

Diante desse cenário, é essencial adotar uma postura mais consciente e estratégica no uso das redes sociais, reconhecendo seus mecanismos de manipulação e buscando formas de consumir informação que estimulem o pensamento crítico. Filtrar conteúdos, diversificar fontes e evitar reações impulsivas são passos fundamentais para escapar da armadilha do engajamento emocional artificial. Além disso, fortalecer o hábito da reflexão e da análise aprofundada pode transformar as redes em ferramentas de aprendizado e debate genuíno, em vez de meros espaços de distração e polarização.

Em vez de sermos reféns da lógica do espetáculo digital, podemos ressignificar nossa relação com essas plataformas, utilizando-as para fomentar diálogos construtivos e fortalecer a consciência coletiva. A internet oferece um vasto potencial para a disseminação de conhecimento e mobilização social, mas cabe a cada um decidir se será um agente ativo nesse processo ou apenas mais um espectador passivo do fluxo incessante de estímulos superficiais. A escolha entre distração e engajamento significativo está, em grande parte, em nossas mãos.

No fim, as redes sociais refletem a forma como escolhemos interagir com o mundo. Se permitirmos que a lógica do entretenimento raso e da indignação instantânea domine nosso tempo e atenção, estaremos apenas reproduzindo o ciclo do "Pão e Circo" digital. Mas, se optarmos por utilizá-las como espaços de troca inteligente, aprendizado e reflexão, podemos transformá-las em arenas não apenas de disputa emocional, mas também de construção de um pensamento mais crítico e autônomo.

Chapter 10
The Role of the Media

The media's influence on society goes beyond simply informing, becoming an active agent in the construction of narratives, setting the public agenda, and emotionally manipulating the masses. Since the early days of mass communication, media outlets have shaped the way people perceive reality, assign importance to certain events, and position themselves in the world. With the advancement of technology and the strengthening of large media conglomerates, this power has intensified, transforming information into a product shaped by economic, political, and ideological interests. The impact of this structure goes beyond entertainment and directly influences public debate, the formation of collective opinion, and citizen participation. In the context of the "Bread and Circuses" phenomenon, the media acts as one of the main instruments to keep the population distracted, emotionally engaged in superficial themes, and oblivious to deeper, structural issues.

Controlling the flow of information allows the media to select, amplify, or omit events, shaping the collective perception of what is relevant. This process, known as agenda-setting, defines the themes that dominate public debate, influencing not only which issues will be discussed but also how they will be interpreted. While sensationalist headlines and exhaustive coverage of sporting events, celebrity scandals, and superficial political conflicts dominate the news, structural issues such as social inequality, environmental degradation, and systemic corruption are often sidelined or addressed in a simplified way. This direction of collective attention keeps society trapped in cycles of momentary outrage, volatile emotions, and pre-fabricated narratives, diverting focus from deeper problems that would require critical reflection and concrete action.

Beyond the choice of topics, the media also manipulates the way information is presented, resorting to the spectacularization of facts, the exploitation of primary emotions, and ideological polarization. The incessant search for audience and engagement leads to sensationalist approaches, where shock, controversy, and dramatization replace balanced analysis. In a media environment dominated by alarmist headlines and heated debates, rationality gives way to impulsive reactions, making the population more vulnerable to manipulation and less likely to seek in-depth knowledge. Given this scenario, the development of critical thinking and media literacy becomes essential for people to be able to interpret information independently, identify patterns of manipulation, and resist the logic of empty entertainment that sustains contemporary "Bread and Circuses."

The media, in its primary function of informing, has the power to set the public agenda, determining which themes and events will be considered relevant by society. This ability to select and highlight certain information to the detriment of others makes it a strategic force in the construction of the perception of reality and in the definition of social priorities. In the context of "Bread and Circuses," the media often uses this power to prioritize themes that generate emotional appeal and mass engagement, to the detriment of more complex, relevant issues that require critical reflection.

Whether through newspapers, magazines, radio, television, or digital platforms, media narratives are carefully constructed to keep the public emotionally engaged in themes that, in practice, hardly change their lives. Sensationalist headlines, extensive coverage of sporting events, glamorous awards, reality shows, and celebrity gossip occupy a disproportionate space in the news, while themes such as social inequality, environmental crises, public health problems, and political challenges are often sidelined or addressed superficially.

Sensationalist headlines are one of the main resources used to attract attention and generate immediate emotional engagement. Appeals to fear, outrage, and morbid curiosity are common in headlines that shock or alarm, even when the content of the news does not justify this tone. This strategy contributes to the creation of a hyper-stimulating and superficial informational environment, where emotional impact overrides the search for accurate information and in-depth analysis.

Coverage of sporting events and awards also occupies a significant space in media programming, especially on TV and digital platforms. The spectacularization of sports, the creation of epic narratives about competitions and athletes, the exaltation of rivalries, and the cult of victory are strategies that generate passion, fanaticism, and emotional identification in the public. Similarly, awards such as the Oscars, the Grammys, and the Golden Globes have become large-scale media events that mobilize millions of viewers around the world and fuel celebrity culture and the pursuit of status. Although they have cultural and artistic value, these events often receive disproportionate attention, diverting focus from urgent and relevant issues for society.

The media also plays a crucial role in intensifying social polarization, stimulating rivalries, and transforming rational debates into passionate clashes. Political coverage, in particular, is often based on ideological polarization, the personalization of conflicts, and the simplification of complex issues. Media outlets often take opposite positions on the political spectrum, shaping their narratives for specific audiences and reinforcing the confirmation bias of readers and viewers. This type of polarization fragments public debate, hinders dialogue, and intensifies animosity between groups with different views.

The dissemination of fake news and distorted information, driven by social media and amplified by the speed of the internet, further aggravates this scenario. Fake news, rumors, and conspiracy theories, often created to manipulate public opinion or generate emotional engagement, find fertile ground in networks, where they spread rapidly and reach millions of people. The difficulty in distinguishing reliable information from false information, coupled with the overload of content and the polarization of public debate, undermines trust in traditional media and leads many to resort to alternative sources, not always verified.

It is worth noting that criticizing the media's role in the "Bread and Circuses" phenomenon does not mean ignoring its complexity or generalizing its impacts. The media ecosystem is diverse, composed of different outlets, journalists, and approaches. Not all media production aims at distraction and emotional manipulation. There are spaces dedicated to investigative journalism, critical analysis, and plural debate. However, the dominant logic of contemporary media, driven by the market and by political and economic interests, contributes to the maintenance of the cycle of distraction and emotional engagement.

To escape this manipulation and break the cycle of "Bread and Circuses," it is essential to adopt a more critical and active stance towards information. It is necessary to learn to select reliable and diverse sources, question simplistic and polarized narratives, verify the veracity of information before sharing it, and seek in-depth analysis on topics relevant to society. Developing media literacy—the ability to critically analyze content and understand the mechanisms of information production and dissemination—is an essential tool to avoid manipulation and exercise citizenship in a more conscious and informed way.

Given this scenario, it is essential that each individual takes an active role in constructing their own worldview, instead of simply absorbing the narratives that are presented to them. The media has the power to inform and educate, but also to manipulate and distract. Therefore, it is up to the public to differentiate between content that broadens their understanding of reality and that which merely fuels cycles of empty outrage and superficial entertainment. Seeking diverse sources, practicing critical thinking, and questioning ready-made discourses are fundamental strategies to escape the excessive influence of the media spectacle.

Furthermore, it is necessary to recognize that information is not neutral, but reflects interests and power structures. Understanding the mechanisms that govern the media and the incentives behind content production makes the public less vulnerable to manipulation and more capable of interpreting facts autonomously. This does not mean rejecting the media completely, but learning to use it strategically, taking advantage of its positive aspects without becoming hostage to its logic of emotional engagement and constant distraction.

In the end, the real challenge lies in rescuing the depth of public debate in an environment dominated by superficiality and the ephemerality of narratives. More than passively consuming news and entertainment, it is necessary to cultivate a culture of reflection, dialogue, and the pursuit of knowledge. Only then will it be possible to break with the logic of modern "Bread and Circuses" and transform the media into an instrument of genuine information, instead of a mechanism of control and alienation.

Chapter 11
The Culture of Entertainment

Contemporary society is undergoing a profound transformation in the way entertainment shapes collective perceptions, behaviors, and emotions. Far beyond a simple artistic expression or pastime, it is structured as an industrial and market-driven system designed to capture and direct the attention of the masses. Films, series, reality shows, music, video games, and social networks form an interconnected ecosystem, designed to stimulate emotions, reinforce values, and create engaging narratives that go beyond fiction and infiltrate everyday reality. This phenomenon not only reflects cultural trends, but also shapes them, profoundly influencing how people interpret the world and interact with each other. Modern entertainment is not neutral; it carries intentions, discourses, and strategies that act both consciously and subliminally, promoting ideologies, behavioral patterns, and lifestyles that often escape the public's critical perception.

The culture of entertainment plays a central role in the construction of the collective imaginary, dictating aspirations, desires, and beliefs. Audiovisual productions use universal narrative archetypes to create emotional identification and establish deep connections with the viewer, who projects themselves onto the stories and characters, experiencing vicarious emotions and strengthening symbolic ties with these fictional narratives. Social networks and digital platforms intensify this phenomenon by offering a continuous flow of highly personalized content, designed to maximize engagement and transform entertainment into a constant cycle of emotional consumption. In this scenario, the border between reality and fiction becomes increasingly blurred, and entertainment begins to play a role similar to that of "Bread and Circuses" in Ancient Rome, operating as a large-scale distraction mechanism that keeps the public emotionally engaged, but cognitively disarmed. Easy access to digital entertainment, combined with the irresistible appeal of engaging narratives and audiovisual stimuli, makes this immersion almost inevitable.

The constant presence of entertainment in everyday life directly affects the formation of individual and collective identity. The sense of belonging, which was previously based on concrete social ties and shared experiences, is now mediated by entertainment products that offer an artificial sense of connection. Entire communities organize themselves around fandoms, digital influencers, and fictional narratives, creating an environment where entertainment not only reflects social values, but defines them. This generates impacts that go beyond simple passive consumption, influencing political discourses, interpersonal relationships, and even the way people structure their time and attention. Thus, understanding the culture of entertainment does not only mean analyzing media products, but deciphering the underlying mechanisms that transform it into a tool of social influence, determining how people think, feel, and interact with the world around them.

It is essential to recognize that the culture of entertainment does not arise spontaneously; it is a complex and deliberately structured industry, with specific objectives and well-defined strategies. Films, series, music, and other products are carefully planned to attract and retain audiences, generate profits, and consolidate brands and narratives. This industrial and market-driven character means that entertainment is not neutral or devoid of intentions, but rather a vehicle for messages, values, and ideologies, often implicit, that shape perceptions and behaviors.

At the center of this process is the incessant search for emotional engagement. Films, series, music, and other formats are created to arouse intense emotions, from joy and excitement to sadness, fear, and anger. Technical and artistic resources, such as impactful soundtracks, striking visual effects, and charismatic characters, are used to create immersive experiences that capture attention and keep the audience engaged for long periods. This emphasis on emotion over reason, on sensory experience over critical reflection, is a hallmark of modern entertainment.

The construction of emotional narratives is one of the most effective strategies of the entertainment industry to ensure engagement. Films, series, and reality shows often follow classic narrative archetypes, such as the hero's journey, the clash between good and evil, forbidden romance, and overcoming challenges. These stories, reinvented in different contexts, resonate deeply with the public, arousing feelings of identification, empathy, and catharsis. The emotional connection with fictional characters and imaginary plots is one of the main factors that make the culture of entertainment so engaging.

Furthermore, this culture subtly and persuasively promotes the illusion of belonging. Fandoms, online communities, awards shows, and intense media coverage create a sense of community around fictional products and characters. For many people, especially those who feel isolated or are searching for identity, entertainment offers a space for connection and belonging. However, these ties are largely superficial, based on emotional involvement with external narratives, and not on genuine interpersonal relationships.

Excessive consumption of entertainment also fosters a passive and uncritical attitude towards information and emotional stimuli. Mass entertainment, with its continuous flow of light and emotionally appealing content, requires little cognitive effort and offers instant gratification to the brain. This constant search for easy stimuli can reduce the ability to concentrate, make thinking more superficial, and hinder the understanding of complex information. In addition, passive consumption of entertainment makes individuals more vulnerable to media and social manipulation, as it weakens critical thinking and intellectual autonomy.

Examples of this phenomenon are evident. Reality shows exploit voyeurism and the exposure of private life to generate emotional engagement. Superhero series, with their simplistic narratives and grandiose visual effects, offer escapism and instant gratification, diverting attention from complex social and political issues. Awards shows like the Oscars and Grammys have become high-impact media events, reinforcing celebrity culture and the cult of fame. Popular songs, often with repetitive lyrics and catchy melodies, promote superficial messages and reinforce consumerist values.

The culture of entertainment, by occupying an increasingly large space in people's lives, contributes to the formation of masses emotionally involved in external narratives, but disengaged from truly relevant issues. This passivity, fueled by excessive consumption of entertainment, makes people more vulnerable to strategies of social control and media manipulation, perpetuating the cycle of contemporary "Bread and Circuses".

This chapter sought to analyze how the culture of entertainment promotes the illusion of belonging and influences the behavior of the masses, making them more passive and susceptible to manipulation. Understanding this mechanism is fundamental to developing a more critical and conscious relationship with entertainment products, seeking more authentic and meaningful forms of leisure, culture, and social engagement.

The challenge, therefore, is not only to recognize the influence of entertainment, but to develop a critical eye to differentiate passive consumption from conscious appreciation. This does not mean rejecting entertainment, but rather understanding its impacts and making more deliberate choices about what we consume. The ability to question narratives, perceive intentions, and reflect on the emotions aroused can transform the individual's relationship with media culture, making consumption more balanced and enriching.

Instead of being a passive spectator, the person can take an active role in their experience with entertainment, choosing content that broadens their worldview and stimulates deeper reflections. Rescuing forms of leisure that encourage creativity, genuine social interaction, and critical thinking is essential to balance the impacts of the culture of entertainment on a daily basis. Art, literature, music, and cinema can be more than mere distractions—they are valuable tools for intellectual and emotional enrichment.

Building a more conscious relationship with entertainment is not only the responsibility of the public, but also of the creators and distributors of content. Valuing productions that challenge the viewer, stimulate debates, and encourage reflection can contribute to a richer and more diverse cultural environment. After all, entertainment can alienate, but it also has the power to inspire, educate, and transform. The way we choose to interact with this culture will determine the impact it will have on society and the individual.

Chapter 12
The Cult of Celebrity

The growing influence of celebrities in contemporary society reveals a complex phenomenon, in which public figures go beyond their areas of expertise to become cultural icons, role models, and even objects of worship. Idolatry of artists, influencers, and athletes goes beyond simple admiration for their skills, transforming into an intense emotional involvement, which often approaches devotion. The media and social networks amplify this process, creating a cycle in which the overexposure of celebrities fuels the public's fascination, and this fascination, in turn, further reinforces their visibility. This cult does not happen by chance, but is sustained by a sophisticated media apparatus that exploits human psychology, manipulating desires, aspirations, and the need to belong.

The emotional involvement with public figures intensifies as they cease to be just talents to be admired and become symbols of success, power, and an idealized lifestyle. The public projects themselves onto these personalities, feeling an indirect connection that can fill emotional gaps and reinforce their own identity. In a society marked by individualism and the fragmentation of traditional social ties, celebrity culture becomes a means of symbolic connection, where fans share interests and emotions around their idols. However, this connection is rarely reciprocal, as celebrities remain distant figures, carefully constructed by marketing and public relations teams. Thus, this relationship becomes unilateral, with the public investing genuine emotions in figures who, in most cases, are media characters shaped to meet commercial and cultural expectations.

Social media has intensified this cult by creating a direct channel between fans and celebrities, promoting an illusion of closeness and intimacy. Platforms like Instagram, Twitter, and TikTok allow these figures to share moments of everyday life, making them seemingly accessible and relatable. However, this exposure is, in most cases, calculated and strategically planned to maintain the public's relevance and engagement. The entertainment culture encourages this dynamic by transforming celebrities' personal lives into a spectacle, exploiting dramas, scandals, and moments of vulnerability as media commodities. With this, the cult of celebrity is consolidated as a powerful tool of social influence, not only shaping behaviors and aspirations, but also reinforcing consumption patterns and values that favor the logic of entertainment as a form of control and distraction.

The psychological need to project emotions onto public figures is one of the central drivers of this cult. Human beings are social by nature, with a strong need for connection and identification. In an increasingly complex and individualized world, this need finds an outlet in celebrity culture. Public figures, widely publicized by the media and social networks, become symbols of success, beauty, charisma, and other socially valued attributes. By projecting aspirations and desires onto these personalities, a vicarious emotional bond is created, as if the public were participating, albeit indirectly, in their lives and achievements.

The fascination exerted by celebrities comes, in part, from the idea that they personify ideals that many would like to achieve. Artists represent creativity and public recognition. Influencers symbolize popularity and social influence. Athletes are seen as examples of discipline and overcoming. Following these figures gives the illusion of proximity to these ideals, as if, in some way, the public shared their brilliance and success.

Furthermore, this emotional projection is linked to the search for role models and guidance in times of uncertainty. Celebrities, with their widely exposed lives and carefully constructed narratives, offer patterns of behavior, lifestyles, and values that many fans adopt. For young people in search of identity and belonging, identifying with a celebrity can represent a sense of direction and a group to connect with.

The cult of celebrity manifests itself in various ways, from simply following the lives of public figures to creating deep emotional bonds, which may resemble intimate relationships. Fans dedicate considerable time and energy to following their idols, participating in events, consuming related products, and interacting in online communities. For some, this is a form of entertainment and leisure, but for others, it can take on an obsessive character, affecting their daily lives and interpersonal relationships.

Cases of fans who develop intense emotional bonds with celebrities are widely documented. Passionate letters, extravagant gifts, vigils in front of hotels and residences, invasions of privacy, and even stalking are examples of how this cult can go beyond the limits of healthy admiration and become a harmful obsession. There are fans who experience the successes and failures of their idols as if they were their own, demonstrating how intense and, in some cases, problematic this emotional bond can become.

It is important to emphasize that this phenomenon is intensely encouraged by the media and social networks, which profit from the public's engagement around celebrities. Gossip magazines, TV shows, and entertainment websites constantly fuel interest in the private lives of public figures, exploiting voyeurism, curiosity, and the desire for proximity to idols. This constant and massive media exposure creates an environment in which the cult of celebrity is normalized and amplified.

Social networks play a crucial role in this process. Digital platforms allow celebrities to communicate directly with their fans, reinforcing the illusion of closeness and intimacy. They share moments of their daily lives, interact with followers, and promote their work, creating a carefully crafted public image. For fans, these social networks are a way to express admiration, send messages, and interact with other followers, strengthening the sense of community.

However, this digital interaction can intensify fans' emotional dependence, fueling a cycle of idolatry that makes them even more connected to these figures.

In its most extreme cases, the cult of celebrity can generate harmful emotional dependence. Fans who are overly involved with the lives of their idols may neglect relationships, responsibilities, and personal projects, dedicating disproportionate time and energy to following these public figures. In some cases, their self-esteem and sense of personal worth become tied to the success and approval of celebrities, making it difficult to deal with frustrations and failures in real life. This type of dependence can obscure the importance of building one's own identity and developing authentic and meaningful interpersonal relationships.

This chapter explored the psychological need to project emotions onto public figures and how this global phenomenon, driven by the media and social networks, can generate harmful emotional dependence. Understanding the roots of this cult and its mechanisms is essential to developing a more balanced and conscious relationship with the public figures we admire, prioritizing the construction of our own identity and the pursuit of authentic personal achievements.

Recognizing the influence of celebrities in our lives does not mean denying their cultural importance or their positive impact on various causes and movements. However, it is essential that this admiration does not become a form of self-annulment. Excessive idolatry can distort perceptions, leading to the forgetting that, behind the impeccable public image, there are flawed human beings, subject to mistakes and challenges like any other person. Seeing celebrities with a more critical and realistic view allows for a less dependent and healthier relationship with this universe.

Seeking references and inspiration is natural, but true personal evolution happens when one learns to value one's own trajectory, without the need to live in the shadow of idealized figures. The time and energy invested in the cult of celebrities can be directed towards the development of individual talents, building real relationships, and strengthening self-esteem. After all, admiration does not need to mean submission, and the influence of public figures should not replace the search for authenticity and personal growth.

In this sense, it is up to each one to reflect on the impact of the cult of celebrity on their life and find a balance between entertainment and emotional autonomy. The fascination with public figures can coexist with a critical and independent view, allowing admiration to transform into learning and inspiration, and not into an emotional prison. In the end, the true protagonism must be in one's own story, and not in that of someone seen from a distance, through the screen of a cell phone.

Chapter 13
Fanaticism and Extremism

Fanaticism and extremism are complex phenomena, rooted in the human need for belonging, identity, and security in a world filled with uncertainties and constant change. Although often associated with sports teams or fervent followers of celebrities, these exacerbated forms of devotion go far beyond these contexts, manifesting in political ideologies, religious beliefs, social movements, and even in everyday interactions. The fanatical mind not only passionately defends its beliefs, but also rejects any questioning or opposing view, treating the other not as an adversary, but as an enemy to be fought. This binary thinking, which divides reality between "us" and "them," fuels extremism and can lead to aggressive, intolerant, and, in extreme cases, violent behavior.

In fanaticism, the individual's identity merges with the cause, belief, or leader they follow. For the fanatic, their ideology is not just a choice among several possibilities, but an absolute and unquestionable truth. By identifying completely with a group or idea, they feel they gain purpose, security, and belonging, warding off the fear of loneliness and uncertainty. However, this blind adherence creates a paradox: by seeking stability in a rigid belief, the fanatic becomes a prisoner of their own inflexible vision, unable to accept change or new perspectives. This rigidity requires constant reaffirmation, leading them to reject any criticism and often react disproportionately, with verbal attacks, persecution, and, in more extreme cases, physical violence.

Extremism is an offshoot of fanaticism, in which devotion to the cause intensifies to the point of justifying any means to achieve the desired goals. Extremist movements often resort to demonizing the enemy, creating myths and conspiracy narratives, and appealing to emotion to recruit followers and consolidate their ideology. These tactics are amplified by the use of propaganda and social media, which disseminate radical discourses on a large scale, hindering dialogue and deepening divisions in polarized societies. Confronting fanaticism and extremism requires not only promoting education and critical thinking, but also creating spaces for dialogue and strengthening empathy, allowing people to question their beliefs without it feeling like an existential threat. Only then will it be possible to build a more balanced, tolerant, and open society to the diversity of ideas.

Fanaticism, in its essence, is characterized by an intense and excessive devotion to a cause, person, or ideology, accompanied by strong intolerance of divergent opinions. Fanatical individuals tend to idealize their idols or beliefs, attributing superhuman qualities to them and considering them infallible. Any criticism is perceived as a personal attack, a threat to their belief system and identity. This difficulty in accepting questioning and the refusal to admit flaws generate rigid behavior, which prevents dialogue and critical reflection.

Extremism takes this mentality to an even more dangerous level, resulting in actions that go beyond the limits of tolerance and civility, often culminating in violence. Extremists defend their causes with absolute conviction and justify the use of any means, including physical aggression, to eliminate opponents. This radicalism feeds on the creation of imaginary enemies and the amplification of collective fears and resentments, leading to extreme polarization and total intolerance.

The psychological factors that drive fanaticism and extremism are complex. The search for identity and belonging is one of the main drivers of these phenomena. In an increasingly uncertain and individualistic world, joining a fanatical group can offer a sense of clear identity, purpose, and community. This need for belonging is particularly strong in individuals who feel marginalized or directionless.

Another striking aspect of fanaticism is the fusion of personal identity with an ideology or group. For the fanatic, the group's beliefs become part of their identity, so any criticism is seen as a direct attack on their existence. This fusion explains the emotional intensity and rejection of criticism that characterize fanatics and extremists.

Fear also plays a central role in fanaticism and extremism. Fear of the unknown, of change, of loss of identity, or of external threats are exploited by radical leaders to mobilize followers and justify extreme actions. Fanatical propaganda often spreads rumors and conspiracy theories to generate panic and paranoia, presenting the group as the only protection against exaggerated or invented dangers.

Fanaticism and extremism are not limited to a single area of life and can arise in different social contexts. In politics, ideological fanaticism and the cult of personality can lead to extreme polarization, intolerance, and violence. Throughout history, totalitarian regimes and radical movements have demonstrated the dangers of political fanaticism, which can result in repression, persecution, and even genocide.

In religion, fanaticism can lead to fundamentalism and even terrorism. The history of humanity is full of conflicts motivated by religious intolerance, and religious extremism continues to be a global threat. The literal and rigid interpretation of sacred texts, combined with the demonization of other beliefs, generates persecution and violence in the name of faith.

Even in entertainment, fanaticism can have negative effects. Idolatry of celebrities, although less violent, can lead to obsessive behaviors, invasions of privacy, and emotional dependence. In sports, fanaticism can manifest itself in violence between fans, intolerance between rivals, and aggressive behavior motivated by passion for a team.

The dangers of extremism and fanaticism are wide-ranging. At the individual level, they can lead to mental rigidity, difficulty dealing with diversity, and social isolation. At the collective level, they weaken democracy, fuel violence and intolerance, and threaten peace. History shows numerous examples of tragedies caused by these extreme forms of thought.

Extremism can also be used as a tool of control by authoritarian regimes and radical groups. Disinformation, emotional manipulation, and repression are often employed to silence opponents and impose a single ideology. Control of information, censorship, and the use of force are common strategies of extremist governments to maintain power and eliminate any form of dissent.

To combat fanaticism and extremism, it is essential to invest in education, critical thinking, intercultural dialogue, and the valuing of diversity. Teaching citizenship, promoting debate, and encouraging empathy are essential ways to strengthen people's ability to resist emotional manipulation and build more just and peaceful societies.

Recognizing the influence of celebrities in our lives does not mean ignoring their cultural importance or the positive impact they can have on various causes and movements. However, it is essential that this admiration does not lead to the nullification of one's own individuality. Excessive idolatry can distort perceptions and make one forget that, behind the impeccable public image, there are flawed human beings, subject to mistakes and challenges like any other person. Seeing celebrities with a more critical and realistic eye allows for a less dependent and healthier relationship with this universe.

Seeking references and inspiration is natural, but true personal evolution happens when one learns to value one's own trajectory, without living in the shadow of idealized figures. The time and energy dedicated to the cult of celebrities can be better used in the development of individual talents, in the construction of real relationships, and in the strengthening of self-esteem. After all, admiring does not mean submitting, and the influence of public figures should not replace the search for authenticity and personal growth.

It is up to each individual to reflect on the impact of the cult of celebrities in their life and find a balance between entertainment and emotional autonomy. The fascination with public figures can coexist with a critical and independent view, allowing admiration to be transformed into learning and inspiration, and not into an emotional prison. In the end, the true protagonism must be in one's own story, not in that of someone seen from afar, through the screen of a cell phone.

Chapter 14
The Price of Alienation

Collective alienation imposes a high cost, reflected in various aspects of individual and social life, corroding the authenticity of human experiences and diverting focus from issues essential to personal and collective development. Excessive immersion in manufactured distractions, such as celebrity worship, obsession with media events, and passive adherence to pre-built narratives, distances individuals from themselves, their reality, and their capacity for critical reflection. In a world saturated with superficial stimuli and instant emotional rewards, introspection and the search for a personal sense of purpose in life weaken, making identity and self-esteem increasingly dependent on external factors. Thus, alienation becomes a vicious cycle in which, deprived of autonomy over their own narrative, the individual is content to absorb and reproduce realities imposed upon them.

This detachment from one's own existence has profound emotional impacts, resulting in chronic dissatisfaction, constant frustrations, and an incessant need for stimuli that attempt to compensate for the internal void. By replacing personal challenges and achievements with symbolic victories and vicarious emotions, the individual loses the ability to genuinely fulfill themselves, becoming increasingly susceptible to emotional manipulation promoted by the major entertainment and information industries. This dependence on external factors not only diverts focus from self-realization but also weakens emotional resilience, making people more vulnerable to helplessness and despair in the face of real challenges. Alienation, in this sense, not only pushes fundamental questions aside but also impoverishes emotional life, making authentic experiences less meaningful in the face of the uninterrupted spectacle that promises fulfillment but delivers only temporary distraction.

In the social sphere, this culture of alienation compromises community cohesion and weakens interpersonal bonds, as hyper-connection with external stimuli replaces genuine interaction with others. The fragmentation of human relationships, driven by the prioritization of media narratives over concrete experience, results in a society increasingly individualistic and disconnected from its real collective needs. Furthermore, by focusing energy on manufactured debates, artificial rivalries, and events irrelevant to their daily lives, individuals become less likely to question power structures and seek effective changes that can positively impact their reality. Alienation, therefore, not only diverts attention from urgent issues but also functions as a control mechanism, perpetuating inequalities and hindering the construction of a more conscious and engaged society. Recognizing this cost and regaining autonomy over one's own attention and energy is an essential step to break this cycle and reclaim the protagonism of one's own life.

On the emotional level, the price of alienation manifests itself in a range of negative feelings and dysfunctional psychological states. The constant search for external emotions, whether in the consumption of entertainment, celebrity worship, or passionate involvement in sporting and political events, can generate an emotional dependence similar to other behavioral addictions. Individuals who project their emotions onto these events tend to develop tolerance to emotional stimuli, requiring increasingly larger doses of excitement and commotion to feel satisfaction or pleasure. This incessant search for intense emotions can lead to a state of chronic anxiety, irritability, and constant dissatisfaction, since the source of pleasure and reward lies in external and uncontrollable events.

Frustration and disappointment become frequent companions in the lives of those who emotionally alienate themselves in external events. Teams lose, celebrities fall from grace, political movements fail. When self-esteem and sense of personal worth are tied to these external entities, the failure or defeat of others is experienced as personal setbacks, generating feelings of helplessness, hopelessness, and self-devaluation. The difficulty in dealing with failure, intrinsic to the human condition, is aggravated when individual identity dissolves into achievements and defeats that are not one's own.

Emotional alienation can also manifest itself in the difficulty of experiencing genuine and deep emotions in relation to one's own life and interpersonal relationships. Those who are accustomed to living vicarious, intense but superficial emotions, may lose the ability to feel and express authentic emotions in the face of their own challenges, joys, and sorrows. Personal relationships become superficial and distant, empathy and compassion weaken, and the ability to connect emotionally with other people is compromised. Emotional life, paradoxically rich in external stimuli, ends up impoverished and superficial on a personal and intimate level.

In the social sphere, the price of alienation is revealed in the weakening of community ties and the fragmentation of the social fabric. Excessive dedication to external events, driven by the culture of entertainment and celebrity worship, diverts attention and energy from meaningful interpersonal relationships, civic engagement, and participation in community activities that promote social cohesion and collective well-being. Neighbors become strangers, dialogue and cooperation between different social groups become more difficult, and solidarity and a sense of social responsibility weaken.

Social polarization, fueled by emotional manipulation and the dissemination of simplistic and divisive narratives, is another cost of collective alienation. When public attention is focused on manufactured rivalries, superficial debates, and passionate disputes over irrelevant issues, urgent and complex social issues, such as inequality, poverty, violence, and injustice, are neglected or relegated to the background. The ability to build consensus, engage in constructive dialogue, and seek collective solutions to common problems is undermined by polarization and mass distraction, perpetuating a cycle of inaction and social stagnation.

In the economic sphere, alienation is reflected in the neglect of personal and professional development and the perpetuation of inequalities. Many people, by dedicating themselves excessively to following events irrelevant to their reality, end up neglecting their own education, the development of skills, the search for job opportunities, and financial planning. The time and energy spent on passive consumption of entertainment and emotional involvement with external events could be invested in more productive and constructive activities that contribute to personal growth and improve quality of life.

Collective alienation can be used as a tool of social control, keeping entire classes in a state of passivity and conformity. By offering constant distractions, exciting spectacles, and engaging narratives, governments and elites divert attention from the structural issues that perpetuate inequalities and injustices. The illusion of participation and victory in a symbolic world, offered by "Bread and Circuses," functions as an escape valve for social frustrations and resentments, preventing the population from questioning the status quo and seeking significant transformations.

Economically disadvantaged classes, in particular, may be more vulnerable to alienation and emotional dependence on external events. The lack of real opportunities for social advancement, the precariousness of living conditions, and the feeling of helplessness in the face of structural problems lead many to seek emotional refuge in symbolic achievements, such as sporting victories or the success of celebrities. Entertainment, in this context, functions as a form of illusory compensation, offering moments of joy and excitement that contrast with the harshness of everyday reality. This search for emotional escape, although understandable, can perpetuate a cycle of alienation and passivity, preventing individuals from seeking real solutions to their problems and fighting for a more dignified and just life.

Breaking this cycle of alienation requires a conscious effort to regain autonomy over one's own attention and energy. Critical reflection, development of genuine interests, and the search for real connections can serve as antidotes to the passivity imposed by the excess of external stimuli. This does not mean rejecting entertainment or cultural events, but redefining the way we relate to them, ensuring that they are a complement to life, and not a substitute for a full and meaningful existence.

Rediscovering the value of authentic experiences, true interpersonal relationships, and continuous learning strengthens individual identity and restores the ability to act independently and consciously. Cultivating moments of introspection, establishing one's own goals, and developing personal skills are essential steps to regain protagonism over one's own narrative. In a world that constantly seduces with fleeting distractions, finding purpose and meaning in the small and large choices of everyday life becomes an act of resistance and freedom.

In the end, the true price of alienation lies not only in the loss of critical sense or the weakening of social ties, but in the renunciation of the possibility of a more authentic and fulfilled life. By becoming aware of this cost and seeking more enriching alternatives, each individual can, little by little, reconstruct their relationship with the world, becoming less hostage to external distractions and more in control of their own destiny. After all, living fully is not just reacting to what is offered to us, but actively choosing what deserves our attention and dedication.

Chapter 15
The Relationship with Social Class

The relationship between entertainment-driven alienation and the structure of social classes reflects a phenomenon deeply rooted in inequality of opportunity and unequal access to material and symbolic resources. Individuals from economically disadvantaged classes often see entertainment as an accessible and immediate form of pleasure, belonging, and emotional compensation, alleviating, albeit temporarily, frustrations arising from adverse living conditions. In a system where access to quality education, professional development, and social mobility is restricted, identification with external narratives—whether through football, pop culture, or media leaders—becomes a symbolic alternative to personal fulfillment, often denied by concrete reality. Thus, alienation is not merely an individual choice, but a conditioned response to the structural limitations of the social context.

Immersion in mass entertainment often functions as a psychic survival strategy in the face of a daily life marked by precariousness and uncertainty. The feeling of victory when seeing a team triumph, the fervent engagement in media disputes, or the obsession with the lives of celebrities represent forms of compensation for those who rarely experience their own achievements in an exclusionary system. The problem lies not in entertainment itself, but in how this dynamic can reinforce a cycle of passivity and distraction, diverting focus from fundamental issues such as the fight for better living conditions, political engagement, and the pursuit of intellectual and emotional autonomy. This mechanism can be instrumentalized by elites and governments as a tool of social control, promoting superficial contentment and reducing the collective willingness to question and transform reality.

Despite this, it is a mistake to believe that alienation is exclusive to economically disadvantaged classes or that the relationship with entertainment follows a homogeneous pattern within each social stratum. Alienation manifests itself in different forms and intensities, regardless of socioeconomic position, and the challenge is not to eliminate entertainment, but to stimulate a more critical and reflective cultural consumption. Expanding access to quality education, creating spaces that favor the development of intellectual autonomy, and valuing activities that encourage active participation in society are essential measures to break the cycle of distraction and offer more meaningful paths for personal and collective fulfillment. After all, the problem is not in the act of entertaining oneself, but in the unconscious renunciation of one's own ability to build an authentic and engaged life narrative.

The central premise of this relationship is that the lack of real opportunities for social advancement and personal fulfillment can lead individuals to seek emotional refuge in symbolic achievements. Economically disadvantaged classes face structural barriers that limit access to quality education, well-paying jobs, essential services, and full participation in social and political life. The deprivation of concrete opportunities, coupled with the feeling of powerlessness in the face of an unequal system, generates frustration, hopelessness, and the need for emotional escapes that provide some sense of value, purpose, and fulfillment.

In this context, entertainment presents itself as an accessible escape valve. Sporting events, television programs, social media, and other forms of entertainment offer a universe of illusions and intense emotions, which contrast with the monotony and harshness of everyday life. For those facing financial difficulties, lack of prospects, and scarcity of real opportunities, entertainment can be a temporary refuge, a relief from the oppressive reality, and a source of immediate gratification. The excitement of a football game, the glamour of celebrity life, participation in fan communities, and immersion in fictional narratives provide moments of joy and belonging that can, albeit in an illusory and fleeting way, make up for the absence of recognition and fulfillment in real life.

Entertainment, in this sense, acts as emotional compensation, creating the illusion of participation and victory in a world where, in practice, these people often have no significant influence. Rooting fanatically for a team can generate a sense of belonging to a community and the possibility of experiencing, albeit indirectly, triumph and glory. For those who feel marginalized and excluded from the social system, identification with a winning team can offer a sense of value and recognition, a way to experience the success and celebration denied in other areas of life. Similarly, following the lives of celebrities and joining fan communities can create a sense of connection and proximity to success and glamour, contrasting with the harshness of everyday reality.

It is essential to emphasize that this search for emotional refuge in entertainment is not a completely free and conscious individual choice, but rather an adaptive response to adverse socioeconomic conditions and the lack of real opportunities. Individuals from disadvantaged classes are not inherently more prone to emotional dependence on external events, but live in a system that offers them fewer alternatives for fulfillment and recognition. In this perspective, the search for emotional escapes can be understood as a coping strategy to deal with frustration, hopelessness, and the feeling of powerlessness resulting from social inequality.

Governments and elites, throughout history, have frequently used this dynamic to maintain social order and avoid structural questioning. Mass entertainment and the promotion of popular sporting and cultural events can serve as mechanisms of social control, diverting the population's attention from urgent social problems and complex political issues. By offering "Bread and Circuses," governments and elites create a state of superficial contentment and political passivity, reducing the likelihood of protests, revolts, and challenges to the status quo. This strategy, although not always explicitly planned, has a significant impact on the maintenance of inequalities and the stability of power structures.

However, the relationship between social class and the "Bread and Circuses" phenomenon is not deterministic or homogeneous. Not all individuals from disadvantaged classes are equally susceptible to emotional dependence on external events, just as not all individuals from more privileged classes are immune to this phenomenon. Individual factors, such as personality, life history, personal values, and support networks, also influence how each person deals with entertainment and alienation. Furthermore, within each social class, there is a diversity of experiences, expectations, and aspirations, making any generalization simplistic or inaccurate.

Overcoming this cycle of alienation does not mean denying entertainment, but creating alternatives that promote a more balanced and conscious relationship with it. Instead of consuming culture passively, it is essential to encourage production, reflection, and active participation, ensuring that leisure and media engagement do not replace personal development and the pursuit of real change. Access to education, critical art, and opportunities for growth are powerful tools to transform entertainment into an enriching experience, rather than a mechanism of stagnation.

Awakening to this reality requires a collective effort, which involves valuing initiatives that expand the possibilities of intellectual and cultural autonomy, especially for those historically marginalized. The democratization of knowledge, the strengthening of spaces for debate, and the encouragement of critical thinking are fundamental steps to break with the logic of entertainment as mere distraction and re-signify it as a means of learning and genuine connection. After all, the problem is not in the fun or fascination with inspiring narratives, but in the unconscious abdication of one's own ability to interpret, question, and build one's own path.

In the end, true freedom lies not in the absence of entertainment, but in the possibility of consciously choosing how to relate to it. When leisure becomes a complement to life, and not a substitute for authentic experiences and concrete transformations, the individual takes control of their trajectory. Only then does entertainment cease to be an illusory refuge and become a space for expression, learning, and strengthening of individual and collective identity.

Chapter 16
Exceptions to the Rule

The analysis of the relationship between socioeconomic status and involvement with mass entertainment often leads to simplified conclusions, but reality shows that this phenomenon transcends class barriers. Emotional adherence to external events is not exclusive to the economically disadvantaged; on the contrary, successful individuals, even those who enjoy financial stability and professional recognition, also demonstrate a strong inclination towards this type of involvement. This behavior cannot be attributed solely to a lack of prospects or the need to escape a difficult reality, but rather to more complex and universal factors of the human psyche. The desire for belonging, the search for intense emotions, and the need to relieve the pressures of everyday life are fundamental aspects that drive both those who strive for better living conditions and those who have already reached the top of the social pyramid. Thus, the phenomenon of Bread and Circuses should not be seen only as an instrument of distraction for the less fortunate, but as a structural element of human behavior, capable of capturing the attention and engagement of individuals in different contexts and realities.

In the corporate environment, for example, it is common to see highly qualified executives dedicating themselves fervently to sports teams, heated political discussions, or specific cultural manifestations. Even with access to a wide range of leisure options and intellectual entertainment, many find in the passion for external events an emotional refuge. This involvement can be driven by different factors, such as the need to relieve tensions accumulated in demanding routines, the desire for social connection outside the professional environment, and even the natural impulse to participate in collective narratives that generate identity and belonging. The way this manifests itself varies: for some, it is just a balanced hobby; for others, it can become an obsession that influences their daily decisions and behaviors. Understanding these nuances is essential to understanding why even those who possess autonomy and resources are not immune to the attraction of Bread and Circuses.

Furthermore, the cultural and historical impact on the construction of this behavior cannot be ignored. Since antiquity, humans have sought ways to entertain themselves and connect through shared experiences, whether in Roman spectacles, medieval festivals, or the great events of the modern era. Globalization and social media have further amplified this dynamic, making involvement with external events a collective and instantaneous experience. For successful individuals, often pressured by performance expectations and the need to maintain an image of control, this immersion in entertainment can represent an essential escape valve.

The connection with exciting narratives—whether sporting, political, or cultural—offers a sense of active participation in something bigger than the daily routine, allowing them to feel part of a community and, paradoxically, exert some symbolic influence over the events they follow. When considering these issues, it becomes clear that the phenomenon of Bread and Circuses is not restricted to a single segment of society, but is an intrinsic trait of the human experience, shaped by individual, social, and historical factors.

From the outset, it is important to recognize that socioeconomic success does not confer immunity to the influence of Bread and Circuses. Emotional projection onto external events, fascination with mass entertainment, and the search for collective identification transcend class barriers, being part of the human experience in different contexts. Even those who have achieved professional success, accumulated wealth, or occupy prominent positions are not immune to the appeal of emotional distractions and passionate involvement with events that unfold outside their daily lives.

Careful observation of human behavior reveals countless examples of successful people, in various fields, who demonstrate intense involvement with sports, politics, or pop culture. High-ranking executives who fervently follow their teams, renowned investors who participate in heated political debates on social media, and acclaimed artists who passionately express themselves about pop culture are examples of how Bread and Circuses also manifests itself among the most favored. These cases challenge the idea that emotional dependence on external events is a phenomenon exclusive to disadvantaged classes and show the need for a more in-depth analysis of the motivations behind this behavior.

One of the reasons for this involvement, even in successful people, lies in the universal need for escape and stress relief. High-performance individuals, often subjected to intense pressures, constant demands, and great responsibilities, may find in entertainment a way to relax and momentarily disconnect from the tensions of everyday life. Cheering for a team, following a series, or engaging in political debates can serve as a necessary mental break, a breather amidst a demanding and competitive routine. In this sense, Bread and Circuses can be a legitimate leisure activity and a way to preserve emotional well-being.

Another important motivation is the search for social connections and a sense of community outside the professional environment. Successful individuals, often immersed in competitive and hierarchical work contexts, may find in entertainment an opportunity to establish more informal and authentic bonds. Sharing a passion for a team with friends and colleagues, participating in discussion groups about TV series, or engaging in political and social movements can provide a broader sense of belonging, combating the isolation that often accompanies individual success.

However, it is essential to differentiate between healthy involvement with external events and harmful emotional dependence. For successful individuals,

Bread and Circuses is generally integrated in a balanced way into professional and personal life, without compromising performance, relationships, or well-being. The passion for a football team can be just a hobby and a topic of conversation among friends, without becoming a dominant obsession. The balance lies in the ability to keep this involvement within healthy limits, without it becoming an escape from reality or a source of emotional dependence.

On the other hand, when dependence on external events becomes harmful, regardless of social class, Bread and Circuses takes on uncontrolled and obsessive proportions, negatively impacting various areas of life. Excessive dedication to organized fan groups, fan clubs, or radical ideological movements can consume time, energy, and money disproportionately, harming professional responsibilities, interpersonal relationships, and personal projects. In these cases, self-esteem and the sense of personal worth can become excessively tied to the success or failure of external entities, generating emotional instability and difficulties in dealing with one's own challenges.

Psychological, cultural, and historical factors also influence this behavior. Personality traits, such as the search for excitement and the need for belonging, can predispose certain individuals, regardless of their social position, to a more intense involvement with Bread and Circuses. Cultural aspects, such as the valorization of sports and the cult of celebrities, also shape this phenomenon, as do personal experiences and social influences throughout life.

It is essential to recognize the complexity of human motivations and avoid excessive simplifications. Although Bread and Circuses tends to have a greater impact on economically disadvantaged classes, the fact that successful individuals also become emotionally involved with external events shows that this phenomenon transcends class barriers. To understand its impact on human life, it is necessary to analyze each case individually, considering its nuances and particularities.

The human fascination with collective narratives and external events cannot be reduced to a matter of social class or financial condition. It is part of a broader context, where emotional, psychological, and cultural factors play an essential role. The need to connect with something beyond routine, to feel intense emotions, and to share experiences with other people continues to be one of the main drivers of this behavior, regardless of socioeconomic level. Bread and Circuses, far from being just a form of distraction for the masses, reflects a structural characteristic of human nature, shaped by deep needs for belonging and meaning.

However, although this involvement can provide pleasure and connection, there is a fine line between balanced passion and harmful obsession. When attachment to external events begins to consume excessive energy, divert focus from essential responsibilities, or compromise emotional autonomy, it becomes clear that a limit has been crossed. The challenge, then, is not to avoid these forms of entertainment and collective identification, but to find a balance that allows them to coexist harmoniously with other areas of life.

What differentiates healthy involvement from emotional dependence is the ability to maintain autonomy over choices and reactions. Recognizing that entertainment and emotional engagement are part of the human experience does not mean passively accepting their unrestricted influence. On the contrary, understanding the mechanisms that fuel this attraction enables a more conscious and positive use of these elements, ensuring that Bread and Circuses remains a complement to life, and not a factor that governs it.

Chapter 17
The Illusion of Control

The belief that we can influence external events, even without any real control over them, is a psychological phenomenon deeply rooted in human behavior. This illusion of control makes us feel like active participants in events that, in reality, are far beyond our reach. When we passionately root for a team, fervently discuss politics, or obsessively follow a media storyline, we often believe, even unconsciously, that our emotional and intellectual dedication can somehow affect the outcome of these events. This deception, while comforting, masks the true individual powerlessness in the face of complex systems and decisions that occur independently of our will. The illusion of control not only reinforces the attraction to "Bread and Circus," but also keeps us trapped in cycles of emotional engagement that consume time and energy without offering real influence over the results.

The urge to believe that we have control over what happens around us stems from a fundamental psychological need: the search for predictability and order in an often chaotic and unpredictable world. Since the dawn of humanity, the ability to identify patterns and infer causality has been essential for survival.

However, this same cognitive tendency can distort our perception of reality, leading us to believe that subjective actions—such as wearing a lucky shirt before a game or participating in heated debates on social media—have a direct impact on external events. This cognitive bias is widely exploited by media mechanisms and digital algorithms, which reinforce the feeling that every like, comment, or share has a significant weight in the construction of social and political reality. Thus, the illusion that our virtual or emotional participation has a transformative power is fed, when, in fact, our capacity for effective interference is extremely limited in these contexts.

Although the illusion of control can, in some cases, function as a positive stimulus for action and persistence, its excessive presence can lead to frustration and emotional exhaustion. When we become intensely involved with events that we cannot change, we run the risk of diverting our attention from concrete aspects of life in which we, in fact, have control and the capacity for change. Instead of investing energy in unproductive virtual debates or in unfounded hopes that our cheering will make a difference in the score of a game, a more conscious direction towards actions within our real field of influence can provide a more genuine sense of control and fulfillment. The challenge lies in recognizing this illusion and developing a more balanced view of our ability to interfere in the world, focusing on what is truly within our reach.

The root of the illusion of control lies in the human tendency to seek patterns, connections, and causalities, even in situations where chance and randomness play a predominant role. In sports, for example, fervent fans often believe that their emotions, energies, and cheering rituals can influence the outcome of a game. Chants, superstitions, specific clothing, and ritualistic behaviors are adopted in the belief that they can, in some way, propel the team to victory or ward off defeat. This belief, although without a rational or empirical basis, offers an illusory sense of agency and participation in events that, in fact, are defined by a series of factors that escape individual control.

In the political and social field, the illusion of control manifests itself in the belief that participating in heated online debates, disseminating opinions on social networks, or engaging in demonstrations can exert a significant influence on events. Individuals spend hours passionately discussing political issues, sharing news and opinions, convinced that their virtual actions are contributing to social change or the defense of their causes. Although civic participation and political engagement are important and valuable, it is essential to recognize the limits of individual influence in a complex and multifaceted social system. Exaggerated belief in the effectiveness of individual action can lead to frustration, disillusionment, and a sense of powerlessness when the expected results do not materialize.

The media and social networks constantly reinforce this illusion, fueling the belief that participation, engagement, and expression of opinions in virtual public spaces are equivalent to exerting real influence over events. Algorithms prioritize viral content and generate emotional engagement, creating the false impression that popular opinions and online demonstrations have a direct and immediate impact on reality. Media coverage of sporting and political events, often focused on building narratives of heroes and villains and dramatizing conflicts and rivalries, also contributes to this illusion, reinforcing the idea that individuals and groups have significant power to shape the course of events.

The intense emotions aroused by involvement with external events can mask the real powerlessness of the individual in the face of issues that are beyond their control. Passion for sports, political fervor, or moral outrage generate a sense of purpose and engagement that diverts attention from the lack of effective control over the events themselves. Fans feel deeply connected to their teams, political activists become intensely involved with their causes, and social activists commit fervently to their struggles, without, however, exerting a real and direct influence on the sporting results, political decisions, or social transformations they seek. This illusory sense of control, reinforced by intense emotions, can function as a compensatory mechanism, making up for the lack of real control over other areas of life and masking powerlessness in the face of forces and systems that are beyond individual reach.

It is important to emphasize that the illusion of control is not an exclusively negative phenomenon. In certain situations, believing in one's own ability to influence events can be motivating and encouraging, driving action and perseverance in the face of challenges. The conviction that individual effort can make a difference, even in the face of seemingly insurmountable obstacles, is an essential engine of human action and the pursuit of personal and collective overcoming. However, when this illusion becomes excessive, disproportionate, and disconnected from reality, it can lead to frustration, disillusionment, and an even greater sense of powerlessness, in addition to contributing to the perpetuation of the cycle of distraction and emotional manipulation.

Recognizing this illusion and learning to delimit it does not mean giving up passion, engagement, or the pursuit of change, but understanding that not every emotional investment generates real impact. The energy wasted in sterile debates or superstitious rituals can be redirected to areas where individual action really produces concrete consequences. The real challenge is not to give up participating, but to discern where this involvement can be meaningful and productive, avoiding frustrations caused by unrealistic expectations.

By letting go of the exaggerated belief that we can shape the course of uncontrollable events, we open space for another kind of power: that of acting within our own circle of influence. Small changes in everyday life often have a much greater impact than the illusion of influence over complex systems. Instead of wasting energy trying to move impenetrable structures, we can strengthen real ties, build concrete projects, and act in microspheres where our presence and effort generate effective transformations.

More than giving up the desire for transformation, it is about recognizing that true control lies in how we direct our energy and choices. Finding a balance between what we feel and what we can really change allows us to act more consciously, without getting lost in the frustration of trying to control the uncontrollable.

Chapter 18
How to Break the Cycle

Breaking free from the cycle of emotional manipulation and collective distraction requires more than simple awareness; it demands an active effort towards personal and social transformation. Change does not occur spontaneously or automatically, but through a continuous process of re-education, reflection, and deliberate action. To definitively break with "Bread and Circuses," it is essential to recognize the patterns that sustain this dynamic and develop concrete strategies to overcome them. This involves not only understanding the mechanisms of distraction and alienation imposed by mass entertainment and media narratives, but also cultivating an active stance towards information, strengthening intellectual and emotional autonomy. Seeking a more authentic, engaged, and conscious life requires redirecting mental and emotional energy towards what is truly under our control, avoiding wasting time and resources on distractions that contribute little to our development.

The first essential step in this process of rupture is to adopt a solid and independent critical thinking. This means questioning the information received, identifying biases in media discourses, and recognizing strategies of emotional manipulation. In a world where information is abundant, but not always reliable, it becomes essential to learn to differentiate facts from fabricated narratives. To do this, it is necessary to seek diverse sources of knowledge and avoid information bubbles that reinforce pre-existing beliefs without promoting a genuine analysis of the facts. Strengthening critical thinking not only prevents the passive acceptance of biased content, but also broadens one's worldview and enables more informed and autonomous decisions.

In addition to critical thinking, it is essential to develop a more balanced and conscious relationship with entertainment and the media. The consumption of information and leisure should be guided by rational criteria, not by emotional impulses or unconscious habits. This means setting limits on the time dedicated to entertainment content and prioritizing activities that contribute to personal and intellectual growth. Cultivating genuine and productive interests—such as in-depth reading, continuous learning, and engagement in constructive debates—helps to direct focus to more relevant and enriching topics. In this way, the individual not only moves away from the traps of "Bread and Circuses," but also fills their mind with more meaningful experiences, building a life based on authenticity and real purpose.

Education, in its broadest sense, goes beyond the classroom and the simple transmission of factual knowledge. It involves the development of intellectual, emotional, and social skills that enable individuals to critically analyze reality, formulate their own opinions, make conscious decisions, and act ethically and responsibly. In the context of "Bread and Circuses," education focuses on strengthening discernment, logical thinking, and intellectual autonomy, preparing people to be active and critical consumers of information, rather than passive recipients of manipulative messages.

One of the fundamental educational strategies to break this cycle is the development of critical thinking. It allows analyzing information objectively and rationally, questioning assumptions, identifying biases, evaluating the credibility of sources, and recognizing logical fallacies. In the context of emotional manipulation, critical thinking acts as a protective shield, making individuals more resistant to exaggerated emotional appeals, simplistic narratives, and polarized discourses.

To stimulate critical thinking, different educational strategies can be applied at various levels of education. From basic education to continuing education, it is essential to encourage the formulation of questions, the debate of ideas, the analysis of multiple perspectives, and the solution of complex problems. Activities such as analyzing news, deconstructing arguments, identifying biases in discourses, and evaluating the quality of information are essential to strengthen this skill. Critical reading, group discussion, and in-depth research are valuable tools in this process.

Another essential strategy is the development of media literacy. It involves the ability to understand how the media works, how messages are constructed, what their objectives are, and how they can influence our perceptions, beliefs, and behaviors. In the context of "Bread and Circuses," media literacy empowers individuals to critically analyze the content they consume, identify emotional manipulation techniques used by the media, and discern between reliable information and questionable sources.

To develop this skill, it is essential to include in the school curriculum and in continuing education programs activities that encourage the critical analysis of different types of media—newspapers, television, radio, the internet, and social media. Examining sensationalist headlines, misleading advertisements, fake news, and polarized discourses are examples of exercises that strengthen media literacy. In addition, encouraging students to produce their own content—such as videos, podcasts, and blogs—is an effective way to develop a deeper understanding of the mechanisms of production and dissemination of information, as well as promoting a more critical and responsible use of the media.

In addition to critical thinking and media literacy, emotional education plays a fundamental role in breaking the cycle of "Bread and Circuses." It involves developing the ability to recognize, understand, express, and manage one's own emotions in a healthy and constructive way. In the context of emotional manipulation, emotional education helps individuals identify when their emotions are being exploited, regulate impulsive reactions, strengthen resilience, and cultivate emotional intelligence—essential skills to resist exaggerated emotional appeals and make more rational and conscious decisions.

Different pedagogical strategies can be used to develop emotional education, such as self-awareness activities, mindfulness exercises, emotional regulation techniques, simulations of pressure situations, and discussions about emotions and interpersonal relationships. In addition, working on empathy, assertive communication, conflict resolution, and cooperation helps to strengthen emotional resilience and the ability to deal with the challenges of the social world.

Breaking the cycle of "Bread and Circuses" does not mean giving up entertainment or disconnecting from the world, but learning to consume information and leisure consciously, without being led by manipulative narratives or empty distractions. The challenge is not to completely avoid involvement with popular topics, but to develop discernment to realize when we are being guided by irrational impulses and strategically exploited emotions. By practicing mindfulness about what we consume and how we react, we become more selective, investing energy only in what really adds value to our lives and our personal growth.

Furthermore, change does not happen in isolation. Building networks of knowledge exchange, authentic engagement, and enriching debates strengthens both the individual and the collective. Creating environments that encourage and value critical thinking helps to weaken the structures that perpetuate collective distraction and alienation. Small actions, such as encouraging open dialogue, sharing quality content, and promoting constructive discussions, can generate a multiplier effect, making the search for a sharper awareness a continuous and expansive movement.

Breaking this cycle is a daily choice, a continuous process of learning and adaptation. There is no single path or infallible formula, but rather a constant willingness to question, reflect, and act more consciously. As we strengthen our intellectual and emotional autonomy, we become less vulnerable to manipulation and more capable of building a life based on authentic and meaningful choices. In this balance between information, engagement, and discernment, we find true freedom.

Chapter 19
Emotional Minimalism

Emotional minimalism emerges as a necessary response to the excess of stimuli and emotional overload that characterize modern life. In a world where we are constantly bombarded with information, opinions, and external demands, we learn to react impulsively to everything around us, letting our emotional state be shaped by factors beyond our control. This dependence on external stimuli creates a cycle of mental and emotional exhaustion, in which the incessant search for new experiences, debates, or interactions becomes a mechanism of escape and distraction. Emotional minimalism, however, proposes a profound change in this dynamic, teaching us to reduce the influence of these stimuli and to cultivate a more stable emotional state, centered on what really matters for our well-being and personal growth.

The first step towards this transformation is to develop a greater awareness of what triggers our emotional reactions. We often feel that we must react to everything that happens around us—an alarming news story, a social media argument, a sporting event, a distant political conflict. Emotional minimalism, however, invites us to question this need for constant involvement, helping us to differentiate what deserves our energy from what is merely a passing distraction. This conscious filtering does not mean ignoring the world or becoming indifferent, but rather prioritizing emotions that add value to our lives, discarding those that only drain our energy without bringing any real growth.

Another essential aspect of emotional minimalism is building a healthier relationship with our own emotions. Instead of being hostage to emotional impulses triggered by external stimuli, we must learn to recognize and manage our reactions more intentionally. This involves practices such as mindfulness, which allows us to observe our emotions without being dominated by them, and the development of emotional resilience, which strengthens us in the face of adversity. Instead of automatically reacting to every provocation, comment, or external event, we learn to choose our battles and direct our energy towards what really contributes to our growth. In this way, emotional minimalism not only protects us from unnecessary wear and tear, but also allows us to experience a more balanced, meaningful life aligned with our values.

Emotional minimalism, at its core, does not mean suppressing or denying emotions, but rather reorienting our relationship with them. It is not about eliminating the richness and complexity of the human emotional experience, but about directing our attention and energy towards emotions that really matter, those that come from within, reflect our values, and drive our growth and well-being. Emotional minimalism invites us to question the incessant search for external emotional stimuli and to cultivate greater autonomy and self-sufficiency in relation to our emotional life.

This practice begins with a process of self-observation and questioning. It is essential to reflect on the sources of our emotions, identifying to what extent our reactions are triggered by external events, other people's opinions, or media and digital stimuli. Questioning the need to become emotionally involved in heated online debates, ephemeral passions for celebrities, or sports rivalries is a fundamental step to deconstruct patterns of emotional dependence and regain control over our attention and energy.

One of the pillars of emotional minimalism is the conscious filtering of external stimuli. In a world saturated with information and distractions, learning to select what really deserves our attention and energy is essential to avoid mental dispersion. This involves reducing time spent on social media, limiting consumption of sensationalist news and superficial content, and prioritizing activities and information that truly contribute to our growth and well-being.

The practice of emotional minimalism also involves cultivating mindfulness and presence in the present moment. Our mind tends to wander, to worry about the future or ruminate on the past, hindering the full experience of the present and the appreciation of the small joys of everyday life. Mindfulness consists of deliberately directing the focus to the now, observing thoughts, emotions, and sensations without judgment. This practice helps to free us from the cycle of worries and mental distractions, promoting clarity, serenity, and a greater ability to enjoy the present.

Another essential aspect of emotional minimalism is the development of emotional self-regulation. This involves recognizing, understanding, and managing one's own emotions in a healthy way, avoiding impulsive and uncontrolled reactions. This skill is essential to resist emotional manipulation, better deal with stress, and maintain emotional balance in the face of difficulties. Techniques such as conscious breathing, relaxation exercises, meditation practices, and strengthening emotional intelligence are valuable tools to improve self-regulation.

Emotional minimalism is also manifested in simplifying lifestyle and reducing consumerism. Contemporary culture often associates happiness and well-being with the acquisition of material goods and the incessant pursuit of momentary pleasures. Emotional minimalism proposes to reverse this logic, encouraging us to value experiences, relationships, and personal growth instead of accumulating goods or seeking instant gratification. This simplification of lifestyle reduces financial stress, frees up time and energy for more meaningful activities, and promotes more conscious and sustainable consumption.

Another central principle of emotional minimalism is the search for authenticity and coherence with our values. Instead of living to meet other people's expectations or seek social approval, emotional minimalism invites us to live according to our own convictions, to pursue authentic goals, and to express our individuality in a genuine way. This commitment to authenticity strengthens self-esteem, builds a stronger identity, and promotes a life more aligned with who we really are.

Adopting emotional minimalism does not mean turning away from emotions or denying their importance, but learning to live them with greater awareness and balance. When we cease to be hostage to external stimuli and cultivate an internal space of clarity and purpose, we discover that it is possible to feel joy, engagement, and connection without falling into excess or emotional overload. Emotional simplicity allows us to achieve a state of serenity where our reactions are no longer automatic and become intentional, aligned with our true values.

This transformation does not happen overnight, but is a continuous process of detachment from what does not add to us and strengthening of what really matters. Small daily changes, such as consciously choosing which emotional battles are worth fighting, reducing the consumption of toxic information, and practicing mindfulness, contribute to a more balanced and meaningful life. Over time, we realize that we do not need to get involved in every emotional storm around us to feel alive—we just need to learn to value tranquility and silence as genuine sources of well-being.

Emotional minimalism is an invitation to freedom. By reducing mental and emotional noise, we make room for what truly nourishes us: authentic connections, enriching experiences, and a deeper state of presence. By simplifying our emotions, we paradoxically find a richer and fuller life.

Chapter 20
The Power of Self-Responsibility

Emotional self-responsibility is a crucial milestone in building a fulfilling and conscious life. In a society that often transfers blame and delegates well-being to external factors, taking control of one's emotions is an act of true autonomy. This requires each individual to understand that their emotional reactions are not imposed by circumstances or other people, but result from the way they interpret and respond to these influences. Instead of allowing external factors to determine one's emotional state, self-responsibility invites introspection and the strengthening of emotional intelligence, providing a less reactive and more balanced life.

This process begins with the recognition of thought and behavior patterns that perpetuate emotional dependence on external stimuli. Often, people find themselves trapped in cycles of frustration, anger, or dissatisfaction because they believe that their happiness depends on the behavior of others, the success of an external cause, or social validation. However, by accepting that one's emotions are the result of internal interpretations, a path opens for the development of effective emotional regulation strategies. This includes the practice of mindfulness, reframing limiting beliefs, and adopting habits that promote emotional stability. Thus, self-responsibility does not mean ignoring external challenges, but strengthening the ability to face them with clarity and maturity.

By adopting this perspective, the individual is freed from the constant search for culprits and begins to focus on solutions and internal improvements. Self-responsibility allows one to take ownership of one's destiny, eliminating the need to depend on uncontrollable events to feel fulfilled. This state of consciousness not only reduces the impact of manipulative distractions, but also promotes healthier interpersonal relationships, based on authenticity and emotional maturity. Ultimately, true freedom lies not in the absence of external challenges, but in the ability to respond to them with intelligence, balance, and a genuine sense of control over one's life.

Self-responsibility, in its essence, implies recognizing that we are the main architects of our emotional experience. It means abandoning the victim posture, of being a passive receiver of external stimuli, and assuming the role of active agents in building our emotional reality. Instead of blaming the world, circumstances, or others for our feelings, self-responsibility invites us to look inward, to identify our own thought patterns, limiting beliefs, and defense mechanisms that shape our emotional reactions.

Taking responsibility for one's emotions does not mean denying the influence of the external world or ignoring the impact of events and people in our lives. It does mean recognizing that, although we cannot control what happens around us, we have the power to choose how we react to these events. Self-responsibility lies in the ability to distinguish between what is under our control and what is not, focusing our energy on what we can truly transform: our reactions, our choices, and our behaviors.

One of the first steps to developing emotional self-responsibility is to recognize and abandon the tendency to blame others for our feelings. In moments of frustration, anger, or sadness, it is common to attribute to other people or circumstances the responsibility for what we feel. However, this victim stance, in addition to imprisoning us in a cycle of resentment and helplessness, prevents us from recognizing our own role in how we experience our emotions. Self-responsibility invites us to question this tendency, to analyze our reactions, and to identify thought patterns that lead us to certain emotions in the face of external stimuli.

Self-observation and critical reflection on our emotional patterns are fundamental to developing self-responsibility. By observing how we react in different situations, we can identify recurring triggers, dysfunctional thoughts, and limiting beliefs that influence our emotions. This process helps us to understand the roots of our reactions and to see areas of our emotional life that need to be transformed. Self-knowledge, built through self-observation and reflection, is the basis for emotional self-responsibility.

Furthermore, self-responsibility involves developing the ability to regulate one's emotions in a healthy and constructive way. Instead of suppressing or denying emotions, we should learn to welcome, understand, and express them in a balanced way. Techniques such as conscious breathing, relaxation exercises, meditation practices, and strengthening emotional intelligence are valuable tools to improve emotional self-regulation and deal with intense feelings with more awareness and maturity. This mastery over one's emotions helps to avoid impulsive reactions, make more rational decisions, and maintain emotional balance even in challenging situations.

The practice of emotional self-responsibility does not happen quickly or easily. It requires self-awareness, discipline, persistence, and, above all, courage to face emotional patterns and limiting beliefs. It is a continuous process of self-discovery and transformation, which requires patience, self-compassion, and commitment to one's own growth. However, the benefits are immense and transformative. By taking control of our emotions, we gain the freedom of not being hostage to external stimuli, other people's opinions, or manipulative narratives. We develop the emotional resilience to deal with life's challenges, strengthen our interpersonal relationships, and build a more solid and authentic self-esteem.

The journey of emotional self-responsibility is not without challenges, but each step strengthens autonomy and clarity about who we really are. When we stop looking for culprits and start focusing on internal solutions, we free ourselves from emotional dependence on external factors and find a deeper sense of purpose and fulfillment. This process does not mean isolation or insensitivity, but rather cultivating a more balanced relationship with the world, where our emotions are no longer hostage to chance and begin to be directed in a conscious and intentional way.

By developing this ability, we understand that true security is not in the predictability of events, but in the confidence that we can deal with them in the best possible way. Each obstacle becomes an opportunity for growth, and each challenge, an invitation to improve our emotional intelligence. Relationships become more authentic, free from the weight of exaggerated expectations and the need for control over others. Instead of seeking external changes to find peace, we begin to build it within ourselves, understanding that the power to transform our experience has always been in our hands.

Self-responsibility gifts us with the most valuable of freedoms: to live consciously and autonomously, without being dragged by the winds of circumstances. When we take command of our emotions, we cease to be passive spectators of life and become protagonists of our own history, cultivating a balance that allows us to face any storm without losing the essence of what we truly are.

Chapter 21
The High-Performance Mind

The high-performance mind develops from a set of skills, habits, and strategies that allow maximizing human potential in any area. Contrary to the belief that only a few are born with exceptional talents, high performance is the result of a continuous process, based on discipline, a growth mindset, and clarity of objectives. These individuals demonstrate a differentiated level of concentration and self-control, managing to stay focused even in the face of distractions and challenges. In addition to managing their emotions intelligently, they strategically structure their routines, ensuring that each action is aligned with their purposes. The constant pursuit of improvement and the ability to adapt are fundamental characteristics of these minds, allowing them to overcome obstacles and stand out in their fields.

The difference in these people lies in how they perceive and react to everyday challenges. Instead of being carried away by impulses or external stimuli that divert attention, they develop a mental filter that selects only what contributes to their goals. This control does not happen by chance, but results from constant practices of self-awareness, mental training, and structured habits that reinforce resilience and efficiency. While many give in to procrastination or the immediacy of momentary gratification, high-performance individuals understand the value of consistency and continuous effort. In this way, they not only achieve great feats but also sustain high performance over time, transforming challenges into opportunities for growth.

In addition to clarity of objectives and efficient attention management, high performance is directly linked to the ability to regulate emotions and maintain a solid psychological balance. Emotional intelligence allows these individuals to face pressures and adversities without losing stability, making them less vulnerable to stress and demotivation. Instead of allowing negative feelings to limit their possibilities, they use their emotions as fuel for action. This emotional self-regulation, combined with a mindset focused on growth and continuous learning, maintains their motivation and engagement. The pursuit of knowledge and the willingness to reinvent themselves make these people examples of excellence, showing that high performance is not the privilege of a few, but a choice accessible to those who are willing to cultivate the right habits.

Research in psychology and neuroscience indicates that high-performance people share a fundamental trait: the ability to selectively filter external stimuli, focusing attention and energy on what really matters. While most people let themselves be carried away by the incessant flow of information, distractions, and emotional appeals, these minds develop a "mental filter" that allows them to distinguish the essential from the superfluous, the productive from the irrelevant. This mental selectivity is not innate, but a skill cultivated with discipline, self-awareness, and specific practices.

One of the pillars of high performance is clarity of objectives and the definition of priorities. High-performance individuals have a clear vision of their long-term goals and establish well-defined priorities for their daily actions. This clarity acts as a beacon that guides them through distractions, helping them resist the temptation to deviate in search of momentary gratification or irrelevant emotional involvements. Setting priorities helps in the efficient allocation of time and energy, ensuring that mental and emotional resources are directed towards activities that really drive their goals.

Another striking feature is the ability to manage emotions effectively, avoiding impulsive or uncontrolled reactions. High-performance individuals are not devoid of emotions, but they know how to regulate them, using them as a source of information and motivation, instead of being dominated by them. This emotional intelligence allows them to maintain calm and mental clarity in situations of pressure and stress, make rational decisions even in the face of challenges, and persist despite setbacks. Emotional self-regulation is essential for maintaining focus and productivity in the long run.

Discipline and a structured routine are fundamental in the daily lives of these people. Those who achieve success generally follow rigorous routines, with defined times for work, rest, physical exercise, and leisure. This structure favors concentration, productivity, and the maintenance of healthy habits, reducing the chance of procrastination and distractions. Discipline, in this context, is not seen as a restriction, but as an instrument of autonomy, allowing the person to control their time and energy and direct them to what really matters.

The growth mindset is also a common trait among high-performance people. This mindset is based on the belief that skills and intelligence can be developed with effort, dedication, and continuous learning. Individuals with this view see challenges and failures not as insurmountable barriers or signs of lack of ability, but as opportunities for learning and growth. This resilient and optimistic way of thinking allows them to persist in the face of difficulties, learn from mistakes, and maintain long-term motivation. In contrast, the fixed mindset leads to the belief that skills and intelligence are innate and immutable, resulting in fear of failure, avoidance of challenges, and lower resilience in the face of adversity.

The continuous search for knowledge and the development of skills are essential habits of high-performance minds. Those who achieve success are generally tireless learners, always seeking new knowledge and staying up-to-date on advances in their field. This thirst for learning not only keeps them competitive in a dynamic world, but also fuels intellectual curiosity, keeps their minds active, and provides a constant sense of personal evolution.

High performance is not just about achieving great results, but about sustaining a lifestyle based on continuous improvement. This requires a balance between discipline and flexibility, allowing adaptation to different contexts without compromising principles and objectives. True excellence lies not in momentary success, but in the ability to transform each experience into a step towards personal and professional evolution. This commitment to continuous progress makes these minds not only more effective but also more resilient in the face of life's changes and uncertainties.

Furthermore, striving for high performance does not mean being obsessed with perfection. While perfectionism can generate anxiety and self-sabotage, the growth mindset values the process, not just the end result. Learning comes from both successes and mistakes, and those who understand this maintain motivation even in the face of temporary failures. The secret lies in consistency and the willingness to adjust strategies whenever necessary, without losing sight of the purposes that drive them.

Developing a high-performance mind is a personal journey that requires self-awareness, patience, and dedication. It is not a skill exclusive to a few, but a daily construction based on habits, choices, and a clear vision of the future. Those who commit to this transformation not only achieve better results but also find a deeper meaning in their actions, becoming examples of determination, balance, and excellence.

Chapter 22
How to Reprogram Your Mind

Mind reprogramming is an intentional and structured process that seeks to modify thought patterns, limiting beliefs, and automatic reactions that often operate without our awareness. Far from being an abstract or unattainable concept, this transformation is based on neuroplasticity, which proves the brain's ability to create and strengthen new neural connections throughout life. In this way, anyone can reshape their way of thinking and feeling, replacing harmful behaviors with healthier and more constructive mental habits. This process involves identifying beliefs and automatic patterns that keep us trapped in negative emotional cycles, questioning them, and consciously replacing them with more empowering narratives aligned with our personal growth.

The first step to reprogramming the mind is to develop awareness. Many of the thoughts that shape our emotions and behaviors operate automatically and are based on past experiences, cultural influences, and unconscious patterns absorbed throughout life. They determine our perception of reality and influence how we react to the world. Identifying these patterns is essential to interrupt harmful cycles and create space for new ways of thinking. From this recognition, the next stage is to actively challenge beliefs that limit our potential. This can be done through cognitive restructuring, a technique widely used in psychology, which consists of analyzing the validity of a negative thought and replacing it with a more balanced and realistic perspective.

In addition to cognitive restructuring, mental reprogramming is strengthened by practical techniques such as creative visualization, repetition of positive affirmations, and the use of mindfulness. Visualization allows the brain to mentally simulate new behaviors and desired outcomes, reinforcing neural connections that favor real changes. Affirmations help build a new internal dialogue, promoting more empowering beliefs. The practice of mindfulness teaches us to observe thoughts and emotions without being dominated by them, creating a state of presence that facilitates more conscious choices. With the consistent application of these strategies, the mind becomes freer, more resilient, and aligned with the goals that really matter.

Advances in neuroscience in recent decades have revealed that the human brain has a remarkable ability to reshape and adapt throughout life. This neuronal plasticity proves that thought and behavior patterns, even the most ingrained, can be modified through practice, repetition, and new experiences. Understanding the basic principles of neuroplasticity and the functioning of the brain's reward system provides valuable insights into how to reprogram the mind and break vicious cycles of emotional dependence.

One of the central mechanisms of neuroplasticity is repetition. Thought and behavior patterns that are frequently activated strengthen their neural connections, becoming more automatic and habitual. On the other hand, patterns that are rarely used tend to weaken, making room for new connections. This dynamic explains how habits are formed and can be undone. To reprogram the mind, it is essential to identify dysfunctional patterns that reinforce emotional dependence and replace them with healthier and more constructive ways of thinking and acting, through conscious practice and repetition.

Neuro-Linguistic Programming (NLP) offers practical techniques and models for mental reprogramming, exploring the relationship between language, neurology, and behavior. One of the most relevant methods is reframing, or cognitive restructuring, which consists of changing the perspective on a thought, event, or situation, altering its meaning and emotional impact. For example, a thought like "I need the approval of others to be happy" can be reframed to "My happiness depends on me and my self-approval." This practice helps to challenge limiting beliefs, modify negative interpretations, and adopt more positive and empowering perspectives.

Another useful NLP technique is anchoring, which consists of associating a desired emotional state with a specific sensory stimulus, such as a touch, a word, or an image. By creating anchors for positive emotional states – such as calm, confidence, or motivation – we can consciously access them in times of need, assisting in emotional regulation and breaking impulsive patterns. Visualization, another powerful NLP technique, involves creating detailed mental images of yourself experiencing desired emotional states or achieving goals. This exercise strengthens the belief in one's own ability to change and programs the brain for success.

Cognitive psychology also contributes to mental reprogramming through cognitive restructuring, a technique aimed at modifying dysfunctional thought patterns. This method involves identifying automatic negative thoughts, questioning their validity, and replacing them with more realistic and balanced ideas. As our thoughts influence our emotions and behaviors, reframing negative patterns can generate positive changes in the way we feel and act. Socratic questioning, identifying cognitive distortions, and formulating alternative thoughts are useful tools in this process.

The practice of mindfulness also stands out as a valuable tool for mental reprogramming. It consists of directing attention to the present moment, without judgment, observing thoughts, emotions, and bodily sensations as passing events, without identifying with them. Regular practice develops emotional self-awareness, reduces impulsive reactions, and strengthens the ability to observe thoughts and emotions objectively, creating a space for more conscious choices.

To reprogram the mind and break the cycle of "Bread and Circuses," it is essential to adopt an integrated and consistent approach, incorporating techniques from neuroscience, NLP, and cognitive psychology into daily routine. Practical exercises such as questioning automatic negative thoughts, using reframing and emotional anchors, visualizing desired states, practicing mindfulness, and repeating positive affirmations can help modify dysfunctional thought patterns, strengthen emotional self-regulation, and create new neural circuits that sustain a more balanced and resilient mind.

Mental reprogramming does not happen overnight, but is the result of a continuous process of awareness and practice. Small daily adjustments in the pattern of thinking and how we deal with emotions can generate profound transformations over time. The key is consistency and the willingness to replace limiting beliefs with new perspectives that favor personal growth. With patience and commitment, the mind learns to operate in a more positive and productive state, becoming a powerful instrument for achieving goals.

More than modifying thoughts, reprogramming the mind is taking control of one's own narrative and redefining what is possible. As old patterns weaken and new mental habits consolidate, an internal environment conducive to the development of confidence and resilience is created. This transformation reflects not only in the way we interpret the world, but also in our attitudes, relationships, and ability to overcome challenges with balance and clarity.

Reprogramming the mind is a journey of self-discovery that allows us to transcend limitations imposed by the past and embrace a future with more freedom and purpose. When we understand that the brain is malleable and we have the power to direct it towards more constructive paths, we become protagonists of our own evolution. After all, external reality is often a reflection of how we choose to see and interpret it.

Chapter 23
The Art of Detachment

Emotional detachment is essential to achieving balance and inner freedom in a world that constantly pushes us towards dependence on external validation and fleeting rewards. Developing this skill doesn't mean becoming indifferent or insensitive, but learning to experience emotions consciously, without being dominated by them. It's about maintaining relationships, goals, and achievements without letting these factors define your own worth or determine your happiness. When the mind frees itself from the need for absolute control and rigid expectations about the future, it opens space for a more authentic and serene life, where emotions are understood and lived with balance, without the extremes of dependence or denial.

This process requires a deep understanding of the impermanence of life. Everything changes constantly, from everyday experiences to emotional bonds and personal achievements. Becoming intensely attached to something that, by nature, is fleeting inevitably leads to frustration and suffering. Emotional detachment doesn't mean not caring, but accepting changes without resistance, understanding that each experience has its cycle and that trying to hold onto them only generates anguish. Accepting impermanence allows you to value the present without anxiety about the future or regrets about the past, promoting a lighter and more meaningful life.

To cultivate detachment, it is essential to strengthen emotional autonomy and build a sense of worth that does not depend on external factors. When self-esteem is based on solid internal values, the need for validation decreases, allowing for more authentic and conscious decisions. Practices like meditation, mindfulness, and gratitude help in this strengthening, teaching you to observe thoughts and emotions without being carried away by them. True emotional freedom arises when you understand that happiness is not in controlling the uncontrollable, but in the ability to live each moment fully, accepting the transience of life with serenity and confidence.

Contrary to what many think, emotional detachment does not mean an absence of feelings or indifference. In fact, it is the ability to live emotions fully, without being imprisoned by them. It is loving without possessiveness, caring without dependence, and engaging in projects and passions without conditioning happiness on external results. Emotional detachment frees you from the emotional roller coaster imposed by the "Bread and Circus" cycle, allowing for a more balanced and serene life.

One of the fundamental principles of this practice is understanding the transitory nature of all experiences, whether positive or negative. Everything in life is constantly changing, from the seasons to relationships and material achievements. Becoming excessively attached to people, situations, or external results inevitably generates suffering, as impermanence always confronts us with losses, changes, and frustrations. Cultivating this awareness is the first step to developing emotional detachment and freeing yourself from the search for security and happiness in unstable and fleeting sources.

Radical acceptance is another essential tool in this process. Radical acceptance does not mean passivity or conformity, but rather embracing reality as it is, without resistance, judgment, or the desire for things to be different. Fighting against the inevitable and clinging to an unchangeable past or an uncertain future generates suffering and emotional exhaustion. Radical acceptance invites you to embrace the present with openness and curiosity, face challenges with resilience, and find peace by accepting reality as it presents itself.

The development of self-esteem and self-confidence, based on internal values and not on external approval, is also essential for emotional detachment. When a person's sense of self-worth depends excessively on achievements, the opinions of others, or specific results, they become vulnerable to the emotional fluctuations imposed by "Bread and Circus." Building a solid self-esteem, based on internal qualities and self-knowledge, reduces the need for external validation and strengthens the ability to deal with uncertainty and impermanence with more balance.

Meditation and mindfulness are valuable tools for this process. The practice of mindfulness teaches you to observe thoughts and emotions with detachment and objectivity, without identifying with them. This conscious observation allows you to recognize the transience of emotions, understanding that they are only fleeting mental events, and to develop the ability to deal with them with more serenity and less impulsivity. Regular practice strengthens emotional self-regulation, reduces anxiety and stress, and promotes a state of inner peace that favors emotional detachment.

Gratitude also plays a fundamental role in this process. Valuing present experiences, from small everyday joys to great achievements, shifts the mind's focus from the incessant search for more to the appreciation of what already exists. Gratitude teaches you to recognize the abundance of life, reducing the need to always want more or depend on external factors to feel happiness. This habit strengthens emotional resilience, increases psychological well-being, and promotes genuine contentment, facilitating emotional detachment.

Developing emotional detachment requires courage and self-knowledge. You need to be willing to let go of what no longer serves you, accept the natural flow of life, and trust in your own ability to adapt. True emotional freedom arises when we understand that happiness is not in controlling the uncontrollable, but in living each moment fully, without ties to the past or anxiety about the future. This change in perspective allows us to move forward with lightness, embracing experiences as opportunities for learning and growth.

Over time, practicing detachment becomes natural, and inner peace no longer depends on external factors. The suffering generated by the fear of loss or the need for control gives way to a more serene acceptance of reality, allowing for healthier relationships and a more genuine connection with the present. Instead of seeking security in ephemeral things, we begin to find strength within ourselves, cultivating a sense of completeness that is not shaken by the uncertainties of life.

Detachment is opening space for new possibilities, for a more authentic existence, and for a state of true presence. When we stop clinging to what has already fulfilled its cycle, we find freedom to move forward, with a lighter mind and a calmer heart. Detachment does not mean losing, but allowing life to flow more harmoniously, bringing exactly what we need to evolve.

Chapter 24
Creating Your Own Narrative

Building your own life narrative is an act of autonomy and authenticity, allowing each individual to transcend external influences and define a path aligned with their true essence. In a world where pre-packaged stories are constantly imposed by society, the media, and cultural expectations, taking control of one's own trajectory is a gesture of resistance and empowerment. Instead of following scripts that prioritize social acceptance or external validation, creating a personal narrative means setting goals based on internal values, developing genuine passions, and cultivating a solid identity, without depending on superficial symbols of status or success. This process strengthens self-confidence and resilience, while providing a deep sense of purpose and fulfillment.

The construction of this narrative begins with a sincere reflection on what really matters. Often, the directions we follow in life are shaped by inherited patterns or external influences that do not always resonate with our true nature. Questioning these impositions and identifying what sparks genuine enthusiasm is essential to treading an authentic path. This involves recognizing natural talents, exploring deep interests, and defining goals that bring real meaning to existence. When efforts are directed towards goals aligned with personal essence, the growth process becomes more satisfying, and the pursuit of fulfillment is no longer tied to external standards.

In addition to establishing one's own goals and purposes, it is essential to strengthen an identity based on concrete achievements and internal values. The modern world encourages identities built around projected images, social validation, and material achievements that, being external, become fragile and unsustainable. In contrast, a solid identity is anchored in the development of skills, continuous learning, and contribution to something greater than one's own ego. By investing time and energy in building a meaningful trajectory, without depending on external factors to justify its validity, each individual becomes the author of their own story, freeing themselves from the distractions and illusions of "Bread and Circuses" and treading a path of genuine fulfillment.

The construction of a life narrative is a deeply human process and essential for psychological well-being. Since the dawn of civilization, stories have served to give meaning to the world, transmit values, and connect people to a greater purpose. At the individual level, building a personal narrative allows one to organize experiences, integrate past, present, and future in a coherent way, and find a sense of direction and purpose in the journey. When this narrative is authentic and aligned with one's own values, it becomes a shield against the alienation and lack of purpose imposed by "Bread and Circuses."

The starting point for creating this narrative lies in defining authentic and meaningful goals. Instead of following externally imposed goals, social expectations, or desires manufactured by consumer culture, it is essential to reflect on what really matters, which values are non-negotiable, and which goals genuinely resonate with one's own essence. These goals can encompass various areas of life, such as professional development, intellectual pursuits, relationships, health, spiritual growth, and contribution to society. The most important thing is to choose goals that bring genuine inspiration and motivation, providing a sense of fulfillment that goes beyond the search for external validation or momentary gratification.

The development of inner passions also plays an essential role in building a life narrative. These passions are activities, interests, or causes that spark enthusiasm, curiosity, and genuine engagement, providing joy and a natural state of flow. Exploring talents, experimenting with new activities, connecting with deep values, and dedicating time to what generates true satisfaction are ways to discover and nurture these passions. Unlike artificial passions created by "Bread and Circuses," these are authentic sources of motivation and creative energy, bringing a purpose that emanates from within.

The construction of a solid and authentic identity, based on concrete achievements and internal values, is the foundation for sustaining this narrative. Instead of defining identity based on external affiliations, others' achievements, or status symbols, it is essential to develop a sense of personal value anchored in one's own qualities, skills, efforts, and contributions to the world. Developing skills, learning new abilities, overcoming personal challenges, contributing to meaningful projects, and cultivating genuine relationships are ways to build a resilient identity, guided by one's own principles. This authentic identity becomes a beacon amidst life's uncertainties and a shield against external influences and social comparisons.

The focus on personal goals and building a purposeful life significantly reduces the need to cling to external symbols to find happiness and fulfillment. When one is involved in projects aligned with internal values, cultivating genuine passions, and developing an identity based on concrete achievements, the search for external validation and ephemeral distractions loses relevance. Well-being and happiness are then found in the journey of personal growth, in the pursuit of authentic goals, and in living a life aligned with deep values.

Throughout this journey of self-construction, it is natural to face challenges and moments of uncertainty. Creating your own narrative requires courage to question norms, resilience to deal with criticism, and persistence to follow a singular path, even when it seems lonely. But it is in overcoming these obstacles that authenticity is strengthened. Every conscious choice, every step towards a genuine purpose reinforces confidence in one's own trajectory and dissolves the need for external approval, making the process of personal construction even more meaningful.

Over time, this narrative becomes more than a reflection of identity; it also becomes a compass for future decisions. When life is guided by solid values and genuine passions, uncertainties cease to be paralyzing and become opportunities for growth. Thus, the search for an authentic purpose ceases to be a distant ideal and becomes a daily practice, expressed in small actions and choices that resonate with the inner truth of each individual.

Being the author of one's own story is a privilege and a responsibility. It is an act of freedom and, at the same time, a commitment to one's own essence. In a world full of distractions and artificial narratives, those who build their lives with authenticity find a lasting sense of fulfillment, based on what really matters. And, as they write their own stories, they inspire others to do the same, creating a continuous cycle of authenticity and purpose.

Chapter 25
Rescuing Emotional Control

Emotional control is an essential skill for those seeking greater autonomy and resilience, without being held hostage by momentary impulses or the influence of external stimuli. In a world where emotions are constantly manipulated by media narratives, social networks, and marketing strategies, regaining control over one's own mind becomes an act of liberation. Unlike emotional repression, which only intensifies suffering, true emotional control involves understanding, accepting, and directing emotions in a conscious and strategic way. This inner mastery allows one to face challenges with clarity and balance, transforming emotions into allies, not obstacles.

The first step in this process is to develop self-awareness, identifying emotional patterns, recurring triggers, and how certain emotions influence thoughts and behaviors. The practice of mindfulness is a powerful tool for this, as it teaches one to observe emotions without being dominated by them. Conscious breathing exercises, meditation, and emotional journaling help build this inner awareness, allowing for more thoughtful responses in situations that previously would have generated impulsive reactions. Furthermore, questioning automatic thoughts and reframing limiting beliefs are fundamental practices to reduce the impact of negative emotions intensified by distorted internal narratives.

Another essential aspect of emotional control is the regulation of emotional states. Techniques such as cognitive restructuring, positive visualization, and the establishment of emotional anchors help to modify automatic responses and cultivate a more balanced mindset. Instead of allowing fleeting emotions to determine important decisions, emotionally mature individuals use these tools to stay focused on their long-term values and goals. Recovering this control makes it possible to live with more discernment and freedom, without being dragged by the emotional currents imposed by "Bread and Circuses". This continuous process leads to a state of greater mental clarity, allowing for more authentic interactions and choices aligned with a genuine purpose.

Emotional control does not mean repressing or suppressing emotions. It is not about becoming cold or insensitive, but rather about developing the ability to experience them fully without being dominated by them, understanding them as valuable signals and using them as information to make conscious decisions aligned with personal values. Recovering emotional control means transforming emotions from tyrannical masters into useful servants, guiding actions in an intelligent and adaptive way, without being carried away by uncontrolled impulses and reactions.

One of the most accessible and effective techniques for this is the practice of mindfulness. As seen previously, mindfulness consists of directing attention to the present moment in a deliberate and non-judgmental way, observing thoughts, emotions, and bodily sensations as passing events, without identifying with them or being carried away by them. Regular practice strengthens emotional self-awareness, improves the ability to observe one's own internal states with more detachment, and reduces impulsive reactivity, creating space for more conscious emotional choices.

Mindfulness exercises can be easily incorporated into the daily routine, such as seated meditation, mindful walking, attentive breathing, and observation of the senses. Dedicate a few minutes a day to these practices, focusing on your breath, bodily sensations, or surrounding sounds. This helps train the mind to stay present and focused, reducing mental wandering and obsessive rumination on negative emotions. Mindfulness does not eliminate uncomfortable feelings, but allows one to experience them with more equanimity and less suffering, observing them rise and pass like clouds in the sky, without getting attached to them or being dragged by their storms.

Self-reflection is also a powerful tool for strengthening emotional control. Taking time to analyze emotional experiences, identifying triggers, thought patterns, and the consequences of impulsive reactions, generates valuable insights into one's own emotional functioning. Keeping an emotional journal, recording moments of intense emotions, and reviewing them later allows one to develop self-awareness and identify patterns that can be modified.

Furthermore, cognitive control exercises are fundamental in this process. Cognitive restructuring, a technique of cognitive-behavioral therapy, involves identifying negative and dysfunctional automatic thoughts, questioning their validity, and replacing them with more realistic, balanced, and adaptive thoughts. When thoughts like "I'm not good enough" or "Things always go wrong for me" arise, it is possible to question them, look for evidence that contradicts them, and reframe them in a more positive and realistic way, such as "I can learn and improve" or "Not everything goes as planned, but I am capable of dealing with it." Regularly practicing this technique helps to modify dysfunctional thought patterns, reduce the intensity of negative emotions, and strengthen emotional resilience.

The development of emotional intelligence, which involves recognizing, understanding, expressing, and managing one's own and others' emotions, is a continuous and essential process for emotional control. Emotional intelligence is not an innate gift, but a set of skills that can be learned and improved. Reading about the subject, participating in workshops, seeking feedback from trusted people, and practicing empathy and active listening are ways to strengthen this ability and better deal with the complexities of the emotional world.

Rescuing emotional control is not a final destination, but a continuous process of learning and self-discovery. Each challenging experience becomes an opportunity to improve this skill, allowing emotions to be understood and channeled constructively. The more this emotional intelligence develops, the greater the ability to act with clarity, even in the face of adversity. Over time, self-control ceases to be a conscious effort and becomes a natural state, allowing life to be lived with more lightness and purpose.

Besides benefiting oneself, those who learn to manage their own emotions also significantly improve their relationships. Communication becomes more assertive, conflicts are resolved with maturity, and empathy is strengthened. The way we deal with our emotions directly reflects on interactions with others, creating more authentic and healthy connections. Thus, emotional control not only protects against harmful external influences but also enriches life in community.

Recovering dominion over one's own emotions is an act of freedom. In a world that constantly tries to shape reactions and manipulate feelings, developing emotional autonomy is a form of resistance and personal empowerment. When one ceases to be a hostage to impulses and begins to act with awareness and balance, life becomes more meaningful, guided by genuine choices and not by automatic reactions. This is the true power of emotional control: to transform the way one experiences the world, finding serenity even in the midst of chaos.

Chapter 26
The New Model of Thinking

Building a new model of thinking requires a profound shift in how we interpret and react to the world around us. The human mind, often conditioned by automatic patterns and external influences, can be trained to operate in a more conscious and intentional way. This process begins with restructuring how we perceive and process information, replacing impulsive reactions with deliberate responses aligned with our most authentic values. Instead of being carried away by massive distractions and emotional manipulations, we need to strengthen our ability to discern, question, and consciously choose where we direct our attention and energy. This mental transformation doesn't happen immediately but develops with the continuous practice of self-reflection and the pursuit of a clearer, more independent consciousness.

The first step in this change is to cultivate selective attention, which allows us to filter out the excess of stimuli and prioritize what truly contributes to our growth and well-being. In a world saturated with information, where media and entertainment constantly compete for our attention, it becomes essential to distinguish between what is relevant and what is just noise. This implies not only recognizing manipulative and superficial content but also establishing solid internal criteria to define what really deserves our time and involvement. Practicing selective attention doesn't mean ignoring reality or alienating ourselves from events, but adopting a critical and intentional stance on what we choose to consume and absorb. By strengthening this ability, we gain greater control over our thoughts and emotions, reducing the influence of external factors on our mental and emotional state.

In addition to selective attention, adopting an observant mindset is essential for this new way of thinking. Instead of automatically reacting to every emotional stimulus, we can develop the ability to observe our own thoughts and feelings with more detachment and analysis. This doesn't mean suppressing emotions, but understanding them before acting on them. This process helps avoid emotional traps and manipulations, as it allows us to question external narratives and analyze situations with greater clarity. When we combine this observant mindset with a focus on what we can control, we invest our energy more productively, concentrating on concrete actions that really impact our lives and moving away from useless and draining worries. The sum of these elements results in a way of thinking that is more structured, conscious, and aligned with a more authentic and meaningful existence.

This new model of thinking is based on selective awareness, that is, the ability to filter the incessant flow of information and stimuli that bombard us daily, directing our attention to what really matters and discarding the irrelevant noise that only distracts us and prevents us from living with clarity and purpose. Selective awareness doesn't mean ignoring the world, but exercising active discernment about what deserves our attention, where we should invest time and emotional energy, and what we can let pass without harm or deviation from our authentic goals.

At the heart of this selective awareness is the distinction between the essential and the superfluous. In a society that values the ephemeral, the superficial, and the sensational, developing this ability becomes fundamental. Differentiating what is truly relevant to our personal growth, well-being, and realization of values from what is merely distraction, empty entertainment, or manipulative emotional appeal requires self-knowledge, critical reflection, and the courage to question prevailing values and define our own criteria of relevance. What really contributes to my long-term happiness? What activities and information nourish me intellectually and emotionally? Which relationships strengthen and inspire me? Answering these questions honestly and deeply helps us clarify what is essential and filter out what only consumes time and energy without adding value.

The observant mindset is also a fundamental pillar of this new model of thinking. Instead of engaging emotionally in an automatic and impulsive way with external events, this posture invites us to analyze information and stimuli with discernment and objectivity. Having a critical view doesn't mean indifference or lack of empathy, but rather the ability to maintain a healthy emotional distance, avoiding being swept away by momentary passions, fabricated narratives, or manipulative emotional appeals. Observing the world with a questioning eye allows us to identify the mechanisms of "Bread and Circuses" in action, understand the motivations behind emotional manipulation, and resist the influence of harmful distractions.

Focusing on the circle of influence is a practical and powerful principle for applying both selective awareness and the observant mindset in everyday life. Instead of wasting energy and attention on issues beyond our control, such as sports results, distant political decisions, or irrelevant opinions of others, we should focus our efforts on what we can really transform: our own actions, choices, thoughts, and behaviors. By directing our energy to what is within our reach, we increase our sense of control, reduce frustration and helplessness, and expand our ability to generate a positive impact on our lives and the surrounding environment.

The culture of presence complements this new model of thinking, encouraging us to live the present moment with fullness and awareness, instead of getting lost in worries about the future or ruminations about the past. The practice of mindfulness and mindful attention, already explored previously, strengthens the connection with the here and now, allowing us to appreciate the small joys of everyday life and find serenity in the present moment. Living in the present reduces anxiety, minimizes the need to seek future gratifications, and frees us from the incessant search for external stimuli to feel happiness and purpose.

Adopting this new model of thinking means not only changing the way we absorb information, but also transforming the way we make decisions and conduct our lives. When we stop being guided by impulses and external narratives, we start acting with more intention and awareness, choosing paths aligned with our authentic values and goals. This change brings a deep sense of autonomy, as each choice is no longer an automatic reaction and becomes a deliberate step towards a more meaningful life.

Over time, this new mental approach strengthens resilience and clarity in the face of challenges. Instead of feeling overwhelmed by the excess of information and stimuli, we learn to filter what really matters and face adversity strategically. This ability to discern and act with emotional intelligence protects us from the manipulation and distractions of the modern world, allowing us to be the protagonists of our own journey.

Building this new model of thinking is, at its core, a return to the essential: thinking freely, living with presence, and acting with purpose. In a world that pushes us towards distractions and superficiality, developing a more observant and selective mindset is an act of resistance and personal empowerment. The more we cultivate this way of thinking, the closer we get to an authentic life, focused on what really has value and free from the invisible chains of social conditioning.

Chapter 27
The World Without Illusions

The dissolution of the illusions that shape the collective perception of reality would provoke a radical transformation in the way individuals interact with the world and with each other. The veil of distraction, sustained by endless cycles of superficial entertainment and manipulative narratives, obscures clarity of thought and keeps the masses trapped in automatic patterns of behavior. When this veil is lifted, a new consciousness emerges, capable of seeing beyond manufactured distractions and perceiving the invisible structure that governs social dynamics. This change does not happen abruptly, but as a progressive awakening, in which people begin to question accepted truths, critically examine the information they consume, and develop a deeper understanding of the forces that shape society.

As this perception expands, society begins to operate on a higher level of discernment and engagement. The energy previously consumed by irrelevant debates and ephemeral emotional stimuli is redirected to activities that drive human and collective development. With less room for ideological manipulation and rampant distractions, individuals exercise more refined critical thinking, filtering out what truly contributes to their personal evolution and discarding what merely keeps them inert. The impact of this phenomenon manifests itself in all spheres of life: in interpersonal relationships, in the level of awareness applied to choices, and in the ability to build more effective solutions to the challenges faced.

However, this transition does not occur without resistance. Structures that benefit from disinformation and distraction exert a strong influence on maintaining the status quo, and breaking with these patterns requires not only individual effort, but also a collective movement of transformation. Education plays a central role in this process, offering tools for people to develop a critical reading of reality and gain autonomy over their thoughts. At the same time, media and institutions are challenged to act with greater transparency and ethics, as a more conscious population demands greater responsibility from those who shape the public narrative. Although a world completely free of illusions seems utopian, the continuous search for clarity, authenticity, and discernment represents a viable path for the construction of a more lucid, rational, and truly engaged society.

In a world without illusions, social productivity could reach unprecedented levels. Imagine a population no longer consumed by hours of superficial entertainment, heated debates on irrelevant topics, or fleeting passions that add nothing to life. This energy, time, and attention previously wasted on distractions would be redirected to productive activities, personal and professional development, the search for innovative solutions to society's challenges, and the creation of a more prosperous and sustainable future. The creative and productive potential of humanity, freed from the shackles of distraction, would be exponentially amplified, driving advances in all areas, from science and technology to art and culture.

Social consciousness would also rise dramatically. Individuals freed from emotional manipulation and disinformation would develop a more critical and objective view of reality, questioning manufactured narratives, identifying hidden agendas, and demanding transparency and accountability from their leaders and institutions. Public debate would be guided by reason, evidence, and respect for diverse opinions, instead of being dominated by polarization, sensationalism, and inflammatory rhetoric. Civic participation would become more informed and engaged, with citizens aware of their rights and responsibilities, active in the search for solutions to community problems, and committed to the collective well-being.

A society without illusions would be much less susceptible to manipulation. Emotionally mature populations, endowed with critical thinking and resistant to superficial emotional appeals, would be more difficult to control through deceptive advertising, demagogic political speeches, or fake news. The ability to discern and the search for verified information would strengthen collective immunity against disinformation, making society more resilient to attempts at social control and more likely to make decisions based on reason and the public interest, rather than being influenced by fleeting emotions or manufactured narratives.

The culture of entertainment would also be transformed in this new scenario. Leisure, fun, and moments of relaxation would continue to be part of the human experience, but would no longer be used as tools of distraction and manipulation. Entertainment would prioritize content that stimulates creativity, reflection, learning, and authentic connection between people. Art, sports, and leisure would be valued for their potential to enrich life, promote well-being, and strengthen social ties, rather than being exploited as mechanisms of mass distraction and feeding empty passions.

The challenges to achieving a society without illusions would be immense, but not insurmountable. The resistance of economic and political interests that profit from distraction and manipulation, coupled with the inertia of ingrained cultural patterns and the complexity of human nature, would represent significant obstacles. The transition to a more emotionally mature society would require a collective and continuous effort, involving changes in education, media, politics, and culture. The promotion of critical thinking, media literacy, emotional education, and the valorization of reason and evidence would be fundamental steps in this process of transformation.

Achieving a world completely free of illusions may be an unattainable utopia, but the pursuit of this ideal represents a promising path to a better society. Even gradual advances towards greater awareness, discernment, and resistance to manipulation would already bring significant benefits to the quality of individual and collective life. Imagining a world without illusions is not only an exercise in futurology, but an invitation to reflection and action in the present, encouraging us to question our own patterns of thought and behavior, resist emotional manipulation, and contribute, each in our own way, to the construction of a more conscious, rational, and humane society.

Even if a world totally free of illusions seems distant, each individual who awakens to this new perception already contributes to the collective transformation. When someone decides to question imposed narratives, abandon empty distractions, and act with greater awareness, they become a point of light in the social fabric, inspiring others to do the same. Small acts of clarity and discernment, multiplied over time, can generate waves of change that, little by little, reshape the way society operates.

Resisting manipulation and seeking a deeper understanding of reality are not easy tasks, but they are essential for an authentic and meaningful life. The more we cultivate the autonomy of thought, the more we free ourselves from the invisible shackles that condition emotions and choices. This process not only makes us more lucid, but also more responsible for the impact we generate in the world around us. True freedom is not in the absence of challenges, but in the ability to face them with awareness and purpose. The journey to a world without illusions begins within each one of us. By developing a more critical and refined gaze, we strengthen our immunity to manipulation and create a mental space where truth is more valuable than convenience. And, even if illusion never completely disappears, we can choose, day after day, to see beyond it—and that, in itself, is already a powerful form of revolution.

Chapter 28
Breaking Free from the Circus

Breaking free from the "Bread and Circuses" cycle doesn't happen suddenly, but as a gradual process of awakening and inner transformation. True liberation requires a deep commitment to one's own emotional and intellectual autonomy. This path demands courage to question ingrained beliefs, discernment to recognize the traps of distraction, and discipline to build habits that strengthen independent thought. The first step of this journey is to realize the influence that manipulation mechanisms exert on daily life and to understand that passivity in the face of these forces makes us hostage to a system that thrives at the expense of collective alienation.

Throughout this process, it becomes essential to develop a critical eye on the stimuli that consume our attention and energy. Excessive involvement with external events, idolatry of public figures, and the incessant search for superficial entertainment are signs of a disconnection from oneself. Breaking free from this cycle means regaining sovereignty over one's own mind, consciously filtering what deserves or does not deserve to occupy space in our thoughts. This does not mean abandoning leisure or fun, but learning to consume them in a balanced way, without them becoming substitutes for a genuine purpose. True satisfaction does not come from the fleeting excitement provided by momentary distractions, but from building a life guided by authentic values and meaningful achievements.

Emotional independence is the foundation of this liberation. When we stop reacting automatically to external appeals and take responsibility for our own emotions, we become immune to manipulation and social control. This change in perspective allows us to establish more genuine relationships, make decisions more aligned with our essence, and cultivate an inner peace that does not depend on external factors. The world will continue to offer distractions and illusions, but it is up to each one to decide whether to remain trapped in the spectacle or to take the lead in their own existence. The challenge is set: to step out of the role of passive spectator and take control of one's own story, with awareness, purpose, and authenticity.

We revisited the history of "Bread and Circuses," from Ancient Rome to the present day, and found the persistence of this strategy of social control, adapted to each era, but always with the same objective: to distract the masses from essential issues, keeping them passive and susceptible to manipulation. We explored the workings of the human brain and how it can be addicted to external emotional stimuli, understanding the neuroscientific basis of vulnerability to distraction and superficial entertainment.

We analyzed the psychology of crowds and how individual identity can be diluted in the collective, making us more prone to impulsive behaviors and facilitating emotional manipulation in mass events. We reflected on the impact of excessive emotional involvement with external events on identity construction, realizing how this projection can harm self-esteem and personal development, transferring the sense of worth to others' achievements and external symbols.

We unveiled the power of media narratives and entertainment, understanding how carefully crafted stories reinforce the illusion of belonging and emotional identification with external events, diverting our attention from more relevant issues. We analyzed the political use of emotion, observing how leaders and parties exploit fanaticism and polarization to keep the masses controlled, using the same mechanisms of emotional manipulation as entertainment.

We explored the herd effect and how the need for social acceptance can lead us to follow the crowd without rational questioning, making us instruments of social control. We understood how social networks amplified the phenomenon of "Bread and Circuses," creating new arenas of superficial emotional engagement and incessant cycles of distraction, prioritizing content that generates extreme reactions and keeping us trapped in a constant flow of irrelevant stimuli.

We investigated the role of the media in maintaining this cycle, analyzing how sensationalist headlines, sports coverage, and awards ceremonies fuel cycles of excitement and frustration, diverting attention from more relevant issues. We observed the culture of entertainment and how movies, series, reality shows, and events are designed to generate emotional engagement, promoting the illusion of belonging and making the masses more passive and manipulable.

We explored the cult of celebrity, understanding the psychological need to project emotions onto public figures and how this global phenomenon is encouraged by the media and social networks, creating an emotional dependence detrimental to everyday life. We analyzed fanaticism and extremism, examining the psychological factors that lead individuals to defend causes or public figures with irrational fervor and the dangers of extremism as a tool of social control.

We reflected on the price of alienation, investigating the emotional, social, and economic consequences of living by projecting emotions onto external events. We realized how this alienation can be used to keep entire social classes in a state of passivity and conformity. We analyzed the relationship between "Bread and Circuses" and the social structure, noting how the lack of real opportunities can lead people to find emotional refuge in symbolic achievements, and how governments and elites use this strategy to maintain order.

We explored the exceptions to the rule, understanding how extreme involvement with external events can also manifest in successful people, recognizing the complexity of human motivations. We demystified the illusion of control, questioning the belief that cheering fanatically or obsessively discussing a topic exerts real influence over it, paving the way for a more independent and critical mindset.

We analyzed how education can break the cycle of "Bread and Circuses," presenting strategies to develop critical thinking, media literacy, and emotional education, empowering individuals to resist manipulation. We introduced the concept of emotional minimalism, an approach to reduce dependence on external stimuli and live a life more centered on oneself, filtering what really deserves our attention and energy.

Finally, we reflected on the power of self-responsibility, understanding how taking control of one's own emotions is essential to break free from external influences and achieve a fuller and more independent life. We presented a new model of thinking, based on selective awareness, observer mentality, focus on the circle of influence, and the culture of presence, offering a practical guide to a more conscious and balanced life. Finally, we imagined a world without illusions, exploring the potential of a society that is emotionally more mature, productive, conscious, and less susceptible to manipulation.

Now, the final invitation is for you. This book is not an end point, but a starting point. The true liberation from "Bread and Circuses" is not in reading these pages, but in applying this knowledge to your life. The challenge is to awaken to the emotional manipulation of everyday life, to question the imposed narratives, to regain control over your emotions, and to build an authentic life, based on your choices and values.

Break free from the circus. Stop being a passive spectator and become the protagonist of your own story. Disconnect from the incessant distraction, detach from fleeting passions and the search for external validation. Rediscover your talents, explore your passions, define your goals, and pursue them with determination. Build meaningful relationships, invest in your personal growth, contribute to your community, and seek a purpose that transcends the distractions of "Bread and Circuses."

The journey to emotional liberation is challenging, but rewarding. It requires courage to question the status quo, discipline to reprogram the mind, and persistence to stay focused. But the fruits of this journey are invaluable: emotional freedom, mental clarity, inner serenity, authenticity, and a fuller life.

Freeing yourself from the circus does not mean just turning away from manufactured distractions, but reclaiming the right to live with true meaning. The exit from this cycle does not occur through a drastic rupture, but through small daily decisions: choosing reflection instead of reactivity, silence instead of noise, authenticity instead of superficial validation. This process does not eliminate the challenges of existence, but ensures that each obstacle is faced with autonomy and awareness, without emotions being hijacked by external influences.

Every step towards this freedom strengthens a virtuous cycle of clarity and purpose. Over time, what once seemed indispensable—the momentary excitement, the empty disputes, the need to belong to external narratives—loses its shine, giving way to a deeper and more lasting satisfaction. Life becomes less about reacting and more about creating; less about consuming and more about building. The time previously wasted on fleeting distractions is transformed into investment in what really matters: knowledge, authentic relationships, enriching experiences, and the pursuit of self-development.

The question that remains is: what will you do with this newly acquired awareness? Will you remain in the show, surrounded by applause and illusions, or will you decide to step off the stage and take control of your own story? The answer does not need to be immediate, but the call has already been made. Liberation does not happen through a great heroic act, but through the daily choice to live with intention, presence, and authenticity.

Epilogue

After traversing the paths of emotional manipulation, media influence, social projection, and attention control, one essential question remains: what now? What do we do with this knowledge?

Modern society has been built upon a paradox. We live in the information age, yet it has never been more difficult to distinguish the essential from the superfluous. We are encouraged to believe that we are more aware and connected, when in reality, our attention is directed towards carefully crafted distractions. Politics has transformed into spectacle, entertainment into a tool of conditioning, and individual identity into a reflection of dominant trends.

But understanding this mechanism is already a step towards escaping it. And this escape does not require isolation or complete rejection of culture and social interactions. On the contrary, it calls for discernment. It calls for each person to question the stimuli they receive, to recognize when their emotions are being manipulated, and to consciously decide where to direct their energy.

The real challenge is not to eliminate the distractions of the world, but to learn to see them for what they truly are. The problem is not rooting for a sports team, admiring a public figure, or following the news. The problem arises when these experiences become more important than life itself, when identity dissolves into the crowd, and when personal satisfaction depends on events completely unrelated to individual reality.

The final question should not only be "how does the world influence us?", but "what do we do with this influence?". If emotion is the main channel of control of the masses, then emotional autonomy is the key to regaining one's own power. This means developing a more critical view of daily stimuli, valuing authentic experiences, and seeking meaning beyond the spectacle.

There is no simple solution or definitive answer. Each person must find their own balance between engagement and detachment, between participation and reflection. Society will continue to offer new forms of distraction and emotional mobilization, but those who see beyond the surface can navigate this sea without drowning in it.

In the end, the greatest freedom is not the absence of influence, but the ability to consciously choose what deserves our attention, our time, and, above all, our emotion.

www.ingramcontent.com/pod-product-compliance
Lightning Source LLC
LaVergne TN
LVHW040057080526
838202LV00045B/3677